# Green Travel Guide to
# *Northern Wisconsin*

# GREEN TRAVEL GUIDE TO
## *Northern Wisconsin*

### Environmentally and
### Socially Responsible Travel

Pat Dillon *and* Lynne Diebel

THE UNIVERSITY OF WISCONSIN PRESS

The University of Wisconsin Press
1930 Monroe Street, 3rd Floor
Madison, Wisconsin 53711-2059
uwpress.wisc.edu

3 Henrietta Street
London WCE 8LU, England
eurospanbookstore.com

Printed in the United States of America

Library of Congress Cataloging-in-Publication Data
Dillon, Pat (Patricia J.), 1956–
Green travel guide to northern Wisconsin:
environmentally and socially responsible travel / Pat Dillon and Lynne Diebel.
    p.     cm.
Includes bibliographical references and index.
ISBN 978-0-299-28414-5 (pbk.: alk. paper)
ISBN 978-0-299-28413-8 (e-book)
1. Wisconsin—Guidebooks.   I. Diebel, Lynne Smith.   II. Title.
F579.3.D54      2011
917.7504—dc22
2011015960

*To Bob*
— LSD

*To Maura and Nina*
— PJD

# Contents

Contents

# FOREWORD

Among Wisconsin's most popular and authentic attractions are its natural resources, including our northern forests and preserved open space, over 15,000 freshwater lakes, streams and rivers, prime agricultural lands, woodlands, wetlands, and pastures—not to mention outstanding cultural diversity, hip urban environs, and regional specialties. Innovative efforts to preserve these experiences for generations to come are found throughout this comprehensive *Green Travel Guide to Northern Wisconsin*, a companion to authors Pat Dillon and Lynne Diebel's first book on environmentally and socially responsible travel in southern Wisconsin.

The authors take us on an incredible eco-journey where readers discover the diversity, depth, and richness of green tourism in Wisconsin. Protected landscapes, scenic riverways, and recreational trails are described in-depth. Among my favorites are sailing or sea-kayaking around the Apostle Islands, mountain biking on Madeline Island, hiking in Door County's Peninsula State Park, and whitewater rafting on the Peshtigo River near Crivitz.

Pat and Lynne seek out the hidden gems in Wisconsin, including the locally owned hotels, lodges, cottages, restaurants and businesses, exceptional farmers' markets, locally crafted beers and wines, grass-fed beef, heirloom fruits and vegetables, organic dairy, and artisan cheeses. They provide memorable foraging and sustainable dining options that demonstrate the potential of regional food, farm, and restaurant collaboration. Local art, festivals, and events showcase a community's sense of place and people's pride in their cultural heritage. Finally, green technologies—including solar, wind, and bio-fuel sources—demonstrate the potential of clean renewable energy in this state.

*Green Travel Guide to Northern Wisconsin* provides the very best examples of today's "ecopreneurs" who are implementing innovative best practices, technologies, and mindsets to benefit their communities in many ways. At Wisconsin Environmental Initiative, we work with forward-thinking businesses, citizens, and communities to advance the concept of "doing well by doing good." Lynne and Pat have documented businesses that integrate environmental priorities into day-to-day decision-making, many of which are noted as Travel Green Wisconsin certified.

We have a long and proud heritage of environmental stewardship in this state, started by the Native Americans and continued by luminaries such as Aldo Leopold, John Muir, and Gaylord Nelson. It's now time to ask what the next generation of environmental leadership will look like. It could be the businesses, citizens, and communities you read about here. Those who recognize that improved environmental performance can result in a stronger tourism economy, a clean, healthy environment, and a great quality of life.

—JOHN IMES

*Executive Director of Wisconsin Environmental Initiative and*
*co-owner with wife Cathie of Arbor House in Madison, Wisconsin*

# ACKNOWLEDGMENTS

First of all, thank you, Pat, for being a wonderful coauthor. And many thanks to Sheila Leary, Raphael Kadushin, and Adam Mehring of the University of Wisconsin Press for their wonderful support of this book and its older sister, *Green Travel Guide to Southern Wisconsin*, and their invaluable guidance in bringing both to press.

To the farmers, innkeepers, and restaurant owners I visited, thank you for all you do as loyal stewards of the earth. Thank you to Nancy and Steve Sandstrom, and Jon and Danielle Ewalt, in Bayfield, for your vision; to Sarah Renner of Madeline Island, for your restaurant review; to Danette Olsen of Luck for guiding me around the upper Saint Croix River valley and showing me all the wonderful treasures it holds. Thank you to Sisters Johanna and Cecilia at the Christine Center for helping me understand that the Franciscan order has always put earth's best interests at the top of the list. I also thank Charlene Torchia and John Huffaker of Maiden Rock; Marguerite Ramlow, Elizabeth Zenk, Chuck and Mary Egle, and Anello Mollica of Amherst; Sandi Schuettpelz of King; Virginia Smith of Rochester, Minnesota; and Deb and Robert Benada of Rural.

Once again, I thank my son Matt for never tiring of my questions about rivers and lakes, fish, and bicycles; his partner, Rebecca Gass, for her love of Wisconsin forests; my son Greg for his good-natured and expert tech support; and my son James and my daughter Anne, for their enthusiasm from afar. Most of all, I thank my husband, Bob, for his insights, his great photographs, and his unwavering support of yet another book project.

—LSD

Thank you, Lynne. Your honest devotion to restoring and preserving Wisconsin's natural resources gave this book its depth. Thank you to Raphael Kadushin, Sheila Leary, and Adam Mehring of the University of Wisconsin Press for their hard work and support in our belief in traveling with an eco-pilot. Thank you to our copyeditor, Diana Cook, who helped clarify my words. Thank you to my dear friend and editor, Brennan Nardi, who published my first green travel story. To all of my friends and family who held me up through this process—you know who you are. To all of the people throughout Wisconsin who taught me to better understand and appreciate our wonderful natural areas and limited resources. To the makers of our amazing Wisconsin products, I enjoy them more now for knowing who you are and from where they originate. To Maura and Nina, my most precious natural resources, thank you for trusting your mom to navigate during our wild and rustic road trip.

—PJD

# Green Travel Guide to
# *Northern Wisconsin*

Lake Superior

MICHIGAN

DOUGLAS

BAYFIELD

IRON

ASHLAND

VILAS

WASHBURN

FLORENCE

BURNETT

SAWYER

PRICE

ONEIDA

FOREST

POLK

BARRON

RUSK

MARINETTE

LINCOLN

LANGLADE

TAYLOR

ST. CROIX

94

CHIPPEWA

MARATHON

MENOMINEE

OCONTO

DUNN

SHAWANO

PIERCE

EAU CLAIRE

CLARK

PEPIN

PORTAGE

BROWN

KEWAUNEE

BUFFALO

WOOD

39

WAUPACA

OUTAGAMIE

JACKSON

TREMPEALEAU

WINNEBAGO

MANITOWOC

LA CROSSE

90

94

ADAMS

WAUSHARA

CALUMET

MINNESOTA

94

MONROE

90

MARQUETTE

JUNEAU

GREEN
LAKE

FOND
DU LAC

SHEBOYGAN

VERNON

43

SAUK

COLUMBIA

DODGE

OZAUKEE

RICHLAND

94

WASHINGTON

CRAWFORD

90

MILWAUKEE

IOWA

DANE

JEFFERSON

94

GRANT

IOWA

WAUKESHA

94

39

RACINE

LAFAYETTE

GREEN

ROCK

WALWORTH

KENOSHA

0        50 miles

N

ILLINOIS

Lake Michigan

D O O R

# Introduction

What is green travel?

Here's what it means to us.

Green travel is *locally owned lodging* where the innkeepers are committed to continually improving their operations in ways that reduce their environmental impact. Some are Travel Green Wisconsin certified (travel greenwisconsin.com). Some are what we call green-thinking, by which we mean that they continually strive to reduce their environmental impact but have not sought certification. Being green wasn't enough to get in the book—the places we write about are also comfortable and charming.

We ate at *locally owned eateries* that serve local, sustainably grown food as much as possible.

We went *foraging* at farmers' markets, farm markets, and co-ops that sell the truly fresh food grown right in their area. If your lodging has a kitchen, you can cook your own fresh feasts.

We took *farm tours* to see all the exciting, innovative things folks are doing to treat the earth with respect and still earn a living as small farmers, fruit growers, and artisan cheesemakers. We visited community-supported agriculture (CSA) farms, farm share programs that connect people to their food.

To lessen our carbon footprint, we sought ways to *get there and get around by bicycle, on foot, or by public transit*. We found lots of places where you can do just that.

Green travel helps save the great *natural beauty* of Wisconsin that we found in places like State Natural Areas, conservancy land, national and state parks, and quiet little county parks—natural attractions.

We looked for *silent sports*—low-impact outdoor stuff like hiking, biking, canoeing, kayaking, angling, cross-country skiing, snowshoeing, rock climbing, and disc golf—and *low-impact annual events*, all fun ways to enjoy those beautiful places.

We found ways to take home a *new skill*—classes in cooking, art, kayaking, yoga, solar energy, pottery, weaving, and more. Our shopping focused on *local products*, especially local arts and crafts.

Green travel is choosing businesses that take care of their own communities and of the incredible natural beauty that fills every corner of Wisconsin, so that our kids and grandkids will be able to know and love it too.

# Northwest Wisconsin

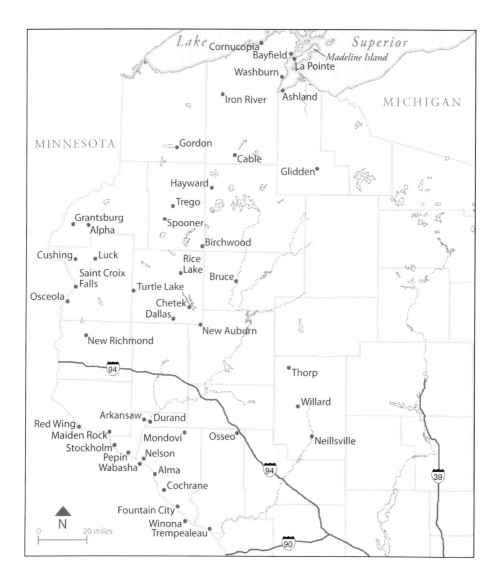

Lake Cornucopia • Superior
Bayfield • *Madeline Island*
Washburn • La Pointe
MICHIGAN
• Iron River • Ashland

MINNESOTA
• Gordon
• Cable
• Glidden
Hayward •
• Trego
Grantsburg • • Spooner
Alpha • Birchwood
Cushing • • Luck Rice
Saint Croix • Lake • Bruce
Falls Turtle Lake
Osceola • Chetek
Dallas
• New Auburn

New Richmond •

94 • Thorp

• Willard
Arkansaw • Durand
Red Wing • Osseo • Neillsville
Maiden Rock • Mondovi
Stockholm • Nelson
Pepin •
Wabasha • Alma 94
• Cochrane 39
Fountain City •
Winona • Trempealeau
N
0   20 miles
90

# By the Inland Sea

## *Bayfield Peninsula Area*

Wilderness to the people of America is a spiritual necessity, an antidote to the high pressure of modern life, a means of regaining serenity and equilibrium.

—SIGURD OLSON, north country conservationist and author

On the Bayfield Peninsula, it's all about nature and being in the outdoors. The area has been a travel destination for inland sea lovers for almost a century. Folks head there all year-round, drawn by the big lake's rugged beauty and Chequamegon Bay's twenty-two-island archipelago. They come in the warm months for the sailing and sea kayaking, for the berry and apple seasons, and for a taste of island life on Madeline. They come in winter for dog-sledding adventures and cross-country skiing, to explore the ice caves, and to cross the bay on the ice road to Madeline.

Along the shore of the Bayfield Peninsula and in the Apostle Islands, the northern hardwood forest meets the boreal forest, and the diverse habitats of this lakeshore and island cluster are home to hundreds of plant species. Several islands provide crucial habitat for nesting and migratory birds. At least thirty-five species of mammals live here. Black bears are common on Stockton, Sand, and Oak Islands and may be seen on any island. Weather and waves have carved the sandstone cliffs of the mainland and islands into beautiful shapes and sea caves, beloved by sea kayakers and ice hikers alike.

The environmental health of the area is vitally important to local Native Americans—the Red Cliff and Bad River Bands of the Lake Superior

Chippewa (Ojibwe). More than 95 percent of the 124,234-acre Bad River Reservation along the shores of Lake Superior remains undeveloped and wild. Members of Wisconsin's Red Cliff tribe, descended from the Madeline Island Chippewa, live on a reservation at the top of the Bayfield Peninsula. Since 1994, the Red Cliff Tribal Fish Hatchery has focused on the reproduction and stocking of indigenous Lake Superior coaster brook trout and walleye, annually restocking more than 750,000 walleye, trout, and whitefish. The Bad River Tribal Hatchery, powered by a wind turbine, focuses on perch and walleye. The Bad River Band also protects the wild rice beds in the Kakagon Sloughs.

In recognition of the area's remarkable beauty and environmental importance, the federal government protected the Apostle Islands and twelve miles of lakeshore in 1970 as a National Lakeshore. The Gaylord Nelson Wilderness permanently preserves 80 percent of the parkland from development. In 2005, the Chequamegon Bay communities of Washburn and Ashland decided that sustainable practices would protect the bay area even more. In 2005, their city councils were the first in the country to pass eco-municipality resolutions, and Bayfield soon followed. Wisconsin's green revolution was quietly born in these small northern towns.

## Getting There

Bayfield is eighty miles from Superior, Wisconsin, which is on the *Greyhound* and *Jefferson* bus lines from Minneapolis to Duluth, and fifty-eight miles from Ironwood, Michigan, which is at the end of the *Indian Trails* bus lines from Milwaukee and Green Bay (with a change of buses in Escanaba, Michigan). Boxed bicycles can be checked under the coach for a fee.

## Where to Stay

Nancy and Steve Sandstrom's *Pinehurst Inn*, a historic mansion with photovoltaic panels and a green-built guesthouse, is green lodging at its best. Once a lumber baron's home, the main house is an imposing shingle-style mansion built in 1885 and known as the Pillar House, for the massive red sandstone pillars that support the front porch. The house is now restored to its original glory, but the solar array by the driveway confirms that it's not the nineteenth century anymore.

From their green-built guesthouse landscaped with native plants, to the biodiesel converter in the garage, to using 75 percent locally sourced organic foods on the breakfast table, Nancy and Steve apply their convictions about

The traditionally styled, green-built guesthouse at the Pinehurst Inn near Bayfield is landscaped with native plants. (photo by Robert Diebel)

sustainable tourism to every aspect of their inn. A recent initiative is to provide Klean Kanteen water bottles for guests to use during their stay (and purchase if they wish). Their business scores top marks—131 points—in the Travel Green Wisconsin program. From the first, they've been active in promoting green tourism. In 2008, the couple coordinated the first Wisconsin Sustainable Business Conference at Northland College in Ashland to offer practical advice on sustainable practices to small businesses.

Their Garden House was constructed with sustainably harvested wood and has fiber cement siding made with recycled wood. The interior trim is red oak from Madeline Island, harvested by hand and transported by horse to reduce impact on the land. Low-flow toilets and showerheads, compact fluorescent light (CFL) bulbs, and a high efficiency boiler reduce energy consumption. Eco-comforts include in-floor hydronic heat, passive solar heat through thermopane windows, solar-heated hot water, Energy Star appliances in the kitchenette, good cross-ventilation for cooling (with backup air-conditioning), and low- or no-VOC (volatile organic compounds) finishes throughout.

Nancy and Steve call their inn "eco-elegant." The four rooms and a three-room suite in the historic Main House and three rooms in the Garden House all have comfy beds, spa robes, and private bathrooms.

Darcy and Michael Schwerin operate the *Enso Wellness Center and Day Spa* in the lower level of the Garden House. They offer massage, body work, facials, and private yoga classes by appointment. The products they use are Spa Technologies (eco-certified, organic seaweed, no parabens, and no phosphates). For winter visitors, Pinehurst has a sauna. And Nancy and Steve serve a yummy breakfast of locally grown foods.

Bayfield visitors can choose from other environmentally conscious lodgings and a campground. The first three described below have full kitchens, encouraging you to shop locally (see Local Foraging) and cook your own feasts.

*Brittany Cottages at Coole Park*, a historic ten-acre estate on Madeline Island, has six cottages, all with full kitchens. The original owners built a formal garden with pergolas and a teahouse in 1920, which was later restored by owners Beth and Alan Fischlowitz, who plan to add a live green roof to the teahouse to reduce runoff. Other eco-friendly initiatives include non-toxic cleaning products and detergents, organic garden fertilizers, and low-flow fixtures and Energy Star appliances in all units. The cottages are located within easy biking distance of the ferry landing.

South of Bayfield, Jeanne and Mike Goodier's *Seagull Bay Motel* has clean, comfortable rooms, reasonable rates, and gorgeous views of Lake Superior. The Guest House, the Cottage, the Residence, and the Walkout have full kitchens. Eco-features include low-flow fixtures, CFL bulbs, highly efficient water heaters and furnaces, nontoxic biodegradable cleaning products, a recycling program, and a towel reuse program. In the interests of good indoor air quality, the Goodiers do not rent to smokers, even those who don't want to smoke in the room. Most units have no air conditioning as they are cooled naturally by lake breezes. Mike said that due to their conservation efforts, "our utility expenses go down every year, and our guests say they like being part of the effort." For their next green initiative, they are working with Focus on Energy on choosing a cost-effective solar installation for hot water.

*Island View Inn and Cottages* is a B&B located on fourteen wooded acres, a mile north of Bayfield, with access to their private beach on Lake Superior. Cottages—open seasonally—have full kitchens. Innkeeper Jeff Shannon makes breakfast with local ingredients—eggs, berries, fruits. Green initiatives include composting (compost buckets in each suite and cottage are emptied daily), rain barrels, CFL bulbs, a recycling program, and non-toxic cleaning products and detergents. And his land is Certified Wildlife Habitat through the National Wildlife Federation.

This one's on Madeline:

Susan and Bob Hartzell's *Inn on Madeline Island* is a collection of rental homes, cottages, and condos with sustainable policies, including energy- and water-saving washing machines, a recycling program (the island recycling program is comprehensive and well run), and linen reuse programs. Their kitchen waste goes to the Madeline Island Community Garden compost pile. Their office has gone paperless, except for contracts. In summer 2011, they began construction of a green-built spa, complete with tents.

These two are located in Bayfield:

The *Bayfield Inn* is located next to the harbor. Conservation measures include earth-friendly detergents and cleaning products, a recycling program, minimal use of paper products (all glassware and china for breakfast service and on the deck bar), low-flow bathroom fixtures, and CFL bulbs. Local products are used whenever possible.

*Harbor's Edge Motel*, located downtown across from the ferry landing, uses CFL bulbs, recycles, and has low-flow fixtures.

Jerry and Mary Phillips's *Rittenhouse Inn* is a bed and breakfast housed in three of Bayfield's grand old buildings. Earth-friendly practices include a recycling program, nontoxic, biodegradable laundry detergents and cleaning products, and the use of local food products and crafts.

This one is between Bayfield and Washburn:

*Artesian House* is an eclectic bed-and-breakfast tucked into twenty-five acres of wooded land and blessed with an artesian well—thus the name. From the first, owner Al Chechik's building was designed with passive solar. In 2008, Paterson Solar of Bayfield installed solar panels, which provide half the hot water. Al also added a native plants rain garden to reduce runoff. Guests are provided with bicycles and bus schedules.

The campground is north of Bayfield:

*Buffalo Bay Campgrounds and Marina* has rustic tent sites at its Point Detour Campgrounds, with spring water, wonderful views, and a stairway down to Lake Superior.

## Where to Eat

For homemade soup, sandwiches, and bakery made with local ingredients, and for a great cup of freshly roasted coffee or Rishi tea, go to *Big Water*

*Cafe and Coffee Roasters*—formerly known as Burt and Francie's. Owners Jon and Danielle Ewalt now roast their beans on-site, thus the new name. And their storefront was expanded and new community tables were built of FSC-certified wood by local woodworker Dave Martinson, who owns the Bayfield business The Woodworks on Manypenny Avenue. Dave also supplies their blueberries from his family's Red Oaks Farm. Keeping it all local, North Wind Organic Farm owner Tom Galazen picks up the cafe's kitchen scraps and coffee grounds weekly—that amounts to about four tons every six months—to enrich his compost. A growing network of local producers drives Big Water's ever-evolving menu. Danielle's bakery goodies—she calls them "rustic gourmet"—include a popular blueberry crumble coffee cake, made with Dave's berries for unbeatable goodness. And her scones are so soft and moist that Jon recommends biting into them blindfolded. Eat in— the newly expanded cafe can seat parties of ten—or order a lunch to go.

The *Rittenhouse Inn's Landmark Restaurant* is open to the public as well as to inn guests. Executive Chef Steve Keen—a graduate of Northland College in Ashland, an avid angler, and an experienced chef—has been with the Rittenhouse since 2009. And he has definitely cultivated the local food scene. Although the yellow fin tuna on the menu is clearly not local, the whitefish and lake trout are right off the boat. Steve's list of local providers also includes NorthStar bison from Rice Lake, Tom Cogger's Maple Hill Farm pork from Washburn, and Morningstar Farm and Vranes Farm lamb. "Returning customers expect seasonal foods and reserve their stay according to what's available," said Steve. In season, about 70 percent of the produce comes from local farmers, with weekly deliveries from providers like Roode Foods Farm in Herbster and Mary Pearson in Port Wing. Beyond all these great ingredients, we like that Steve studied conflict mediation at Northland; a well run kitchen makes for good food.

*Maggie's*, pretty in pink flamingos and other wild decor, is a Bayfield legend and a creation of Mary H. Rice's Flamingos Up North group. To eat locally at Maggie's, order the Lake Superior whitefish, lake trout, or herring. Or try the whitefish livers—an acquired taste. Maggie's offers fun and tasty, somewhat local dining. You'll probably wait in line for a table.

For the Ojibwe, the area's first residents, *manoomin*, or wild rice, was a staple of everyday life. For the Bayfield visitor, dining at Mary H. Rice's nationally acclaimed *Wild Rice Restaurant*, one mile southeast of Bayfield, is a delightful indulgence. The setting—a strikingly simple Scandinavian-style building designed for the wooded lakeshore site by Duluth architect

## Eat Sustainably on Madeline Island

*Lotta's Lakeside Cafe* knows how to satisfy sophisticated palates in comfortable, casual style. Appetizers like "house-smoked organic chicken on wild rice salad with mango vinaigrette," salads of "locally grown chioggia beet salad with feta cheese and a coriander-orange vinaigrette," and entrées like "seared pork tenderloin with hot and sweet tomatillo sauce, fresh corn pancakes, and sautéed local peppers" are the green gift of owner/chefs Chris Wolfe and Janel Ryan.

Popular since its opening in 2000, Lotta's makes a pledge to procure as much locally grown organic food as possible—and it delivers so much more. The ever-changing menu regularly includes chickens, turkeys, eggs, lettuces, vegetables, and chanterelle mushrooms grown by Dick Young of Chanterelle Woods Farm and Good Earth Gardens in Bayfield; fresh-caught trout and whitefish from Bay Fisheries; and field-raised pork from Tom Cogger's Maple Hill Farm in Washburn. Local artists' paintings, basketry, hand-woven rugs, and pottery adorn the interior (and are available for purchase), and fresh flowers from nearby gardens decorate both table and plate. It's the sum of these parts that makes Lotta's the destination for nutritious and delicious dining on Lake Superior's Madeline Island. Beer, wine, and liquors are served.

—Sarah Peet Renner

---

David Salmela—honors its northland locale. *Zizania palustris*, the scientific name of its namesake grain, is honored on hand-painted plates and in the signature Creamy Wild Rice Soup with house-smoked chicken and sautéed Granny Smith apples. When designing his season-driven menus, nationally acclaimed executive chef Jim Webster makes liberal use of local and regional ingredients, including Wisconsin artisan cheeses; regional wild rice; morels that grow on the property; Bayfield County's seasonal apples, pears, berries and veggies; and more veggies from DragSmith Farms in Barron. The staff preserves some of summer's bounty for winter use—such as vacuum-freezing the juice of tasty little Sungold tomatoes for use in soups and sauces. Jim said his entrées are three-quarters regionally sourced. Locals provide Lake Superior whitefish, lake trout, and herring, as well as duck and elk. Northstar Bison near Rice Lake (about

125 miles away) supplies chicken, lamb, and bison. "The bison tenderloin is a top choice for diners, even more popular than the New York strip steak," he said. "The animals are grass fed and finished and humanely raised. I talk to the owner every week." Wild Rice is a bit pricey, but the meals are spectacular, as is its wine collection—primarily California vintages displayed in a centrally located floor-to-ceiling glass cube. Expect a memorable evening.

A visit to Ashland should include historic Chapple Avenue, where you have two outstanding lunch choices. Honore Kaszuba's *Ashland Baking Company* (aka Daily Bread Bakery) has all the ingredients for a picnic: sandwiches made with fantastic breads; desserts to die for, everything from a cookie to a slice of tiramisu; hearty salads; fruit; chips; and beverages. Across the street, the *Black Cat Coffeehouse* serves tasty, mostly vegetarian daily specials and desserts made from scratch with local organic ingredients.

## Local Foraging

If your lodging has a kitchen, you can do your own cooking with local ingredients. In summer and early fall, on Saturday mornings, you can shop at the *Bayfield Farmers' Market*, adjacent to Maggie's in Bayfield; on Mondays and Fridays, at the midday *Washburn Farmers' Market*; on Thursday afternoons, at the *Cornucopia Farmers' Market*, in the park by the beach in Cornucopia; and on Saturday mornings, at the *Ashland Area Farmers' Market*, adjacent to the Chequamegon Food Co-op in Ashland.

Farms and orchards that dot the hills above the lake raise vegetables, berries, fruit, and flowers. The berry cornucopia is filled with strawberries, sweet cherries, juneberries (Saskatoons), tart cherries, gooseberries, raspberries, red currants, blackberries, and blueberries. Fall brings apples, pears, grapes, and plums—pick your own or buy them ready picked. Check the website of the Bayfield Chamber of Commerce (www.bayfield.org) for weekly updates on berry and orchard picking. Almost all area fruit growers use sustainable agriculture methods.

*Bodin Fisheries* in Bayfield, owned by a fourth-generation fishing family, sells fish fresh from the lake—trout, whitefish, herring, and walleye—as well as smoked on-site. They reuse packaging, drive a 2008 ultra-low-sulfur diesel truck, and send their fish waste to a local farmer for compost.

The *Chequamegon Food Co-op*, in Ashland next to the Black Cat Coffeehouse, carries a wide selection of organic foods and products from forty-five local farms, orchards, and other producers—everything from beer and bison to noncultivated wild rice.

### Orchard Sampler

Our favorite orchards and berry farms: *Apple Hill Orchards* has sweet cherries, apples, plums, pears, caramel apples, and apple pies. *Bayfield Apple Company* grows apples and raspberries and makes apple and apple-raspberry cider, jams, jellies, apple mustards, and fruit butters with no added sweeteners. In addition to beautiful views, *Blue Vista Farm* has apples, blueberries, raspberries, fresh-cut and dried flowers, pumpkins, gourds, jams, jellies, salsas, eggs, milk, artisan cheeses, and local crafts. At *Erickson Orchard and Country Store* you'll find strawberries, apples, pears, pasteurized apple cider, apple cider donuts, pies, homemade jams and jellies, apple butter, mustards, and local crafts. *Good Earth Gardens* sells blueberries, currants, blackberries, juneberries (saskatoons), gooseberries, vegetables, herbs, and has a beautiful collection of dried flowers.

### What to Do

Go sea kayaking. There's no better way to experience the beauty of the inland sea. The islands, the sea caves, and the lighthouses are waiting. Plan a multiday trip with camping on uninhabited islands. The *Apostle Islands National Lakeshore* office in Bayfield issues camping permits (required). But don't go until you're experienced in paddling this notoriously dangerous lake. If you're not, have eco-conscious outfitter *Living Adventure* guide you on a day trip or longer—overnight, inter-island trips run from two to seven days. Think luscious beach picnics made with local ingredients. They also offer instruction, kayak rentals, and shuttles. Every other June, the *Inland Sea Kayak Symposium* draws together those who love the lake to paddle, talk, learn, and celebrate, with classes, tours, and seminars for everyone from beginners to experts. As part of the *Lake Superior Water Trail* project, the Inland Sea Society people created a sea kayakers' map of the entire Wisconsin shoreline, showing public access points and campsites.

Sail the archipelago. *Dreamcatcher Sailing*, an environmentally aware Bayfield business with boats anchored at the city dock, will take you on an ecotour for a half-day or on a two-day trip where you anchor overnight by one of the islands. They also teach weekend sailing classes. Their green initiatives include organic food on tours, reusable water bottles, and education about the Lake Superior ecosystem and how to support efforts to protect it.

Be a lighthouse keeper. Volunteer to be a live-in lighthouse docent at the Sand, Devils, or Michigan lights. Applications are due each January, and preference is given to those who can stay three weeks or longer, up to all summer. Volunteers describe the experience as hard work, unforgettable, and highly rewarding. For more information on this and other volunteer opportunities, contact the Apostle Islands National Lakeshore park headquarters in Bayfield or visit the park website.

Bicycle the hills above the lake. You'll find innumerable berry farms, flower farms, and apple orchards (see Local Foraging). The hardwoods are gorgeous in the fall. Rent bikes at Tom Hart's *Bayfield Bike Route*. For a real challenge, bike the fifty-three-mile, very hilly, circle route on Highway 13 and County Road C that takes you clockwise around the Bayfield Peninsula. This route and others are described in the Ashland and Bayfield County Bicycle Map, available at the Bayfield Chamber of Commerce.

Visit the ecologically important *Red Cliff Tribal Fish Hatchery*, open for public tours. Depending on the time of year, you can see brood stock in the raceways, eggs incubating, and fry and fingerlings. And you can learn about the ongoing struggle for a sustainable Great Lakes fishery. It is the only hatchery in the United States to breed the Lake Nipigon strain of coaster brook trout. The *Red Cliff Band of Lake Superior Chippewa* is also part of the ongoing effort to maintain and build the wild lake trout fishery.

Learn to dog-sled. The folks at *Wolfsong Adventures in Mushing* (Dreamcatcher Sailing's alter ego in winter) teach dog-sledding and lead camping trips. Owners John and Mary Thiel also sell Wolfsong Wear, locally made outdoor clothing, online and from their office. The *Apostle Islands Sled Dog Race* in February includes two main events—an eight-dog, eighty-mile race and a six-dog, sixty-mile race—along with a shorter sportsmen's race and a family race. A nice option is to be a "voluntourist"—helping as a dog handler or route guide for the race.

Snowshoeing is big up in Bayfield. The annual Run on Water, an event of the March *Bayfield Winter Festival*, is a five-mile race that offers a chance to snowshoe (or run, walk, or ski) across the bay on the ice highway. Then, to really get into the north country spirit, sign up for the festival's Polar Bear Plunge—through a hole in the ice. After your ice crossing or lake dip, visit one of the event sponsors, the *Bayfield Area Recreation Center*, where the hot tub and indoor pool will warm you up. In late February, Ashland and Washburn also host an ice crossing party, *Book Across the Bay*. Thousands of skiers and snowshoers trek from Ashland to Washburn at night, on a route lit by homemade ice luminaries. It's run by volunteers and the proceeds benefit area residents.

Cross-country ski on forty-two kilometers of groomed Nordic ski trails through old-growth sugar maples, hemlock groves, balsam, and birch woods with views of the Pikes Creek valley, Madeline Island, and Lake Superior. Adjacent to *Mt. Ashwabay Ski and Recreation Area* (summer home of the Lake Superior Big Top Chautauqua) are trails on land owned by Bayfield County that includes the Nourse Sugarbush State Natural Area. The county acquired the last parcel with the help of a Knowles-Nelson Stewardship Program grant. The Bayfield Regional Conservancy website, www.brcland.org, has more information.

Explore the *Nourse Sugarbush State Natural Area* on foot, skis, or snowshoes. From the Mt. Ashwabay Ski and Recreation Area parking lot, follow the Sugarbush Trail about two miles northwest to the Nourse Sugarbush tin shed and cabin. Maple sugaring has been done here for hundreds of years—the Ojibwe tapped the large trees, and diagonal slash marks from early sap collecting are still visible on some trees. Its 480 acres of old-growth northern forest on the northwest flank of Mt. Ashwabay are habitat for the rare black-throated blue warbler.

## Why Is Chequamegon Bay Red?

You may notice that the shallow end of the bay near the visitor center and Ashland turns a murky red at times. We talked with Wisconsin DNR research limnologist Matthew Diebel, who said, "During big rain events, North Fish Creek near the visitor center dumps massive amounts—an average of 17,000 *tons* per year—of red clay and sand into the bay. What you see happening is a relic of old land use processes—clear cutting and log drives that altered the creek channel. The land is in the process of healing, but it will take awhile. Forests regrow in a span of decades, but the channel and banks of North Fish Creek may take thousands of years to recover from the damage." He added that in recent years, the Wisconsin DNR, the University of Wisconsin–Madison, and the United States Geological Survey have been working to reduce this erosive effect by diverting creek flow away from banks with the most potential for erosion.

Head to Madeline Island (*Madeline Island Ferry Line* is Travel Green Wisconsin–certified) with your bicycle and ride up-island to *Big Bay State Park*. Within the park, the 420-acre *Big Bay Sand Spit and Bog State Natural Area* contains a quaking sphagnum-sedge bog. An extensive cordwalk allows visitors to explore the area without disturbing sensitive vegetation. Two state-threatened plant species are found on the site: linear-leaved sundew and coast sedge. The Natural Resources Foundation of Wisconsin (www.wisconservation.org) offers a fall paddle and hike field trip in the park.

Visit the *Northern Great Lakes Visitor Center* two miles west of Ashland to learn more about the area's cultural and natural history. Climb the five-story observation tower and walk the boardwalk interpretive trail. Chat with one of the friendly volunteers to learn all about this beautiful building's many creative eco-friendly features. The center is open every day from nine to five and admission is free.

*Local Arts*

Each July Fourth weekend, the *Red Cliff Pow-wow* takes place across from Isle Vista Casino on Highway 13. On the third weekend in August, the *Bad River Pow-wow* is held east of Ashland on Highway 2 in Odanah.

On the Red Cliff Reservation north of Bayfield, native owned and operated *Native Spirit Gifts and Gallery* is housed in a log building next to the Spur station on Highway 13. You'll find locally made birchbark baskets, beadwork, Bad River wild rice and local maple sugar, books, music, and cultural displays.

A whole book could be written on the Madeline Island arts community. Start your island arts exploration at *Woods Hall Craft Shop*, the retail shop of a weavers and artisans collective. The *Madeline Island Historical Museum* schedules several events each summer celebrating Ojibwe heritage, where tribal artists show their work. The new and thriving *Madeline Island School of the Arts* on historic Sandstrom Dairy Farm offers classes in painting, drawing, fiber, and other arts. Students have on-campus lodging, with breakfast and lunch included in class fees.

And speaking of books, *Apostle Islands Booksellers* is a full-service indie bookstore across from Big Water Cafe and Coffee Roasters in Bayfield. Owners Theron O'Connor and Demaris Brinton's collection includes an amazing range of titles about the history and cultures of the area, as well as a nice selection of new releases, fiction, nonfiction, and children's books.

On Second Street in Bayfield, visit the store with the cobblestone court-yard, *What Goes 'Round*, a small, seasonal independent bookstore owned by Anne Rumsey and Nathan Meyer. They specialize in used books and treasures, such as a hand-colored plate from an 1898 atlas, and carry a selection of new titles as well.

*Bayfield Heritage Tours* are walking tours with attitude. Try the award-winning "Ghosts and Legends of Old Bayfield"—not for the faint of heart.

From mid-June to early September, take in a show at *Lake Superior Big Top Chautauqua*. Performers entertain in a 900-seat, all-canvas tent theater at the base of Mt. Ashwabay ski hill. On warm summer nights they lift the sides and people sit outside. The 2011 schedule included Greg Brown, Arlo Guthrie, Dar Williams, Rickie Lee Jones, and many others, as well as the annual Indian Night. Take the free shuttle bus from Bayfield or the free reserved-seating-only shuttle bus from Washburn.

Heading down-peninsula to Washburn, you'll find community theater, music, dance, and film events year-round—as well as a great view of the lake—at *Stage North Theater*, once the old Swedish Lutheran Church. The annual *Big Water Film Festival* is held here.

In Ashland, walk the old downtown to see seven historic murals painted on brick buildings by artists Kelly Meredith and Susan Prentice Martinsen. Have lunch at the Black Cat, pick up a picnic at the Ashland Baking Company, or grab a vegan sandwich at the Chequamegon Food Co-op. On the south side of town, tour Northland College's *Sigurd Olson Environmental Institute* (SOEI) to learn about Sigurd Olson's life and the mission of the institute. (Sigurd Olson attended Northland College.) You can be a voluntourist with SOEI's LoonWatch program: donate your photography or volunteer as a citizen scientist for loon research projects. Every five years, SOEI coordinates a one-day Wisconsin Loon Population Survey of 250 northern lakes; for those thinking long-term, volunteer Loon Rangers will be needed for the 2015 survey. Voluntourists can also help with boat ramp monitoring for invasive species; "Stop Aquatic Hitchhikers" is part of the Sigurd Olson Legacy Program. There's more. Starting in 2012, SOEI's Adventure Conservation program will schedule a series of great paddling and hiking excursions linked with conservation projects. Trips will be by voyageur canoe, by sea kayak, by canoe down rivers, and hiking the North Country Trail. For example, participants will paddle the Marengo River in the morning, and then work on shoreline restoration in the afternoon.

On the east edge of Ashland, *Timeless Timber* sells quartersawn lumber and finished products made from logs that sank in Lake Superior during the logging boom of the nineteenth and early twentieth centuries. Salvaged from the icy water and low oxygen environment that preserved them, the wood from these logs is an eco-sensitive alternative to harvesting standing forests. Their wood is certified by Scientific Certification Systems. You can explore the retail lumber sales warehouse or shop for smaller pieces in the gift shop.

# Happy Trails

## Cable and Hayward Area

When the axe came into the forest, the trees said, "The handle's one of us!"

—Anonymous

Environmentalists will tell you that the 858,400-acre Chequamegon side of the Chequamegon-Nicolet National Forest, our nation's most heavily logged forest, is an endangered resource. The Wisconsin tourism industry promotes its vast acreage of hardwoods, its 800-plus freshwater lakes, and its 44,000 acres of wilderness areas for almost every sport under the forest canopy. However it's framed, it is a beauty and everyone's responsibility to keep it that way. And what makes it even more remarkable is that the great Northwoods was nothing more than an overlogged, treeless wasteland as recently as the early twentieth century. When immigrants couldn't afford to farm it following the Great Depression, it ended up in the hands of the federal government. Considered one of the greatest conservation success stories in the world, it's also the rope in a tug-of-war among tree-huggers, tree-managers, tree-cutters, and tourists.

The Chequamegon Forest is a prime setting for scads of sports enthusiasts who come from all over the U.S. to bike and ski its trails and paddle its waterways. There's more than enough room for them all with its two hundred miles of trails for nonmotorized use that include two National Scenic Hiking Trails: the North Country Trail and the Ice Age Trail. The town of Cable, on the west side of the forest, is the starting point of the annual American Birkebeiner held in February. The rest of the winter, cross-country skiers use the paths, which are known to be, like Birkie racers, in great shape before the event but understandably sluggish afterward. Mountain bikers have their own place to burn some rubber on the trail system of the Chequamegon Area Mountain Bike Association (CAMBA). These routes give you fat tire riders over three hundred miles to think about nothing more than that rare black bear or timber wolf sighting, the deer that forage the roadsides as if they own them, the speed of your bike, and the tunnel of hardwoods flashing past at breakneck speed. Cable hosts a fat tire event to put your wheel and sprockets to the ultimate test.

If it's paddling in primitive settings that makes you a happy camper, the Chequamegon-Nicolet Forest has over six hundred miles of rivers and streams, many of which flow today as they did before the European settlers brought the timber industry north.

The area has a few ways to eat locally and sustainably, be it sitting at a cafe run by a baker inspired to set up shop directly across from where, as a child, her grandparents lived; or staying where you dine while sampling the fruits of the local laborers. And while the pork may not come from the region, the real meat and potatoes behind Famous Dave's, a story that started in Hayward and is still franchising around the globe, puts this philanthropic Native American on the map as a guy who made great ribs and has a huge heart for helping his people.

You can visit the Cable Natural History Museum to learn how it uses the land to cool down or warm up the building, and how to responsibly use the Northwoods and its delicate and diverse ecosystem.

### Where to Stay

The short drive up to the *Cable Nature Lodge* does not prepare you for what's inside. Set in the Chequamegon-Nicolet National Forest just outside Cable, the lodge is an unassuming but handsome cedar and knotty pine structure set just a few yards back from County Road M. But what's going on inside surprises.

Guests are greeted by owner Bill Brakken, a sixth-generation Cable resident, and his black Labrador, Callie. Both are enthusiastic, with Brakken proud to walk you through his Travel Green Wisconsin–certified lodge to discuss what he's brought to his hometown. His philosophy follows the basic principle of sustainability: live without compromising the ability of future generations to do the same. Brakken opened this lodge as a Northwoods leader in a movement to change the direction in which people

Callie greets guests at the Cable Nature ecolodge. (photo by Pat Dillon)

use Wisconsin's natural resources for recreation—with less impact on the land and more use of local, sustainably made and grown products.

The inn currently utilizes ultra-efficient furnaces and water heaters, low voltage lighting, and nontoxic solvents, and a solar water-heating system is on the drawing board. Each of its seven rooms is spacious but sparsely furnished, luxurious but not lavish. Native plantings and a patio garden are part of the outdoor landscape. And finally, Brakken's restaurant, the Rookery Pub, furthers the cause of a green travel experience with its commitment to the slow food movement and use of local growers.

For recreation, Brakken promotes silent sports by providing information on nearby trails that can be negotiated on foot or bike and lead to a canoe or kayak landing. North Twin Lake Trails or the Rock Lake Trails are less than a mile east of the lodge. But guests who want to stay closer to home have Cable Nature Lodge's twenty-two acres of ungroomed trails on which to hike or snowshoe, with one trail that leads to North Twin Lake.

The lodge acts as a gallery for the work of Lake Geneva photographer Kristen Westlake, featuring color-drenched canvas prints of wildlife caught in motion—birds eating berries, cranes taking flight. Westlake's images reveal her own passion and respect for nature.

## Where to Eat

*The Rookery Pub* was built with lumber from Duluth Timber Company, which specializes in reclaimed wood. Its floors are made of highly renewable bamboo—few new trees were cut for this project. And equally important is that Brakken has made green cuisine available in the Northwoods through the creative culinary vision of his chef, Mike Baxley, who uses local sources almost exclusively. Baxley's menus bring diners closer to the people who grew or raised the entrée's ingredients. He chooses to rotate the menu with the seasons, such as using early spring asparagus for soup or making corn chowder in late summer.

With no deep fryers in the kitchen, the pub satisfies Friday night fish lovers with a "Fish Un-Fry," using fish flown in fresh each week from sustainable fisheries around the world that www.blueocean.org and www.montereybayaquarium.org recommend. Through its commitment to quality, the pub has become popular with seasonal residents and year-rounders, a Cable best-kept secret that's now getting out.

As a fourth-generation Cable resident, Heather Ludzack chose downtown Cable as a logical spot to set up shop after she took the rave reviews from a large wedding she catered very seriously. She and her husband, Larry, opened the *Brick House Cafe* directly across the street from where her grandmother lived. Ludzack now runs this top-notch cafe utilizing farmers' markets and a farm co-op for locally grown produce that she can't find in town. Her goal is to can up the surplus from area farms during the growing seasons so she'll have access to their produce year-round. But Ludzack doesn't stop at conventional methods of obtaining fruits and veggies. She sometimes sends cafe workers out to forage for berries, and uses local syrup she receives in return for her help among the maples during sugaring time. Brick House Cafe and Catering serves up three meals a day, but Ludzack's forte is confections. She claims that she can make any cake in the world ("unless you want it to look like Miller Park"—though she's willing to try!). Go there for an exclusive on grandma-style scones to dunk in possibly the best coffee in town. Brick House Cafe is open for breakfast and lunch, private parties, and catering year-round, for dinner in summer months.

*The Original Famous Dave's* original location is at the Grand Pines Resort on Round Lake outside Hayward. But what makes Dave Anderson's business green has little to do with what's made him famous. His is a story of social responsibility and it is remarkable. Through hard work and perseverance, and his success as a self-made mega-restaurateur, Anderson has gone on to help at-risk Native American teens in a big way. Today Anderson, a registered Chippewa and Choctaw tribal member, isn't quite as casually famous for his Lifeskills Center for Leadership, a life-changing program for teenagers and young adults, as he is for his barbecued ribs, but he should be. Even if his pork doesn't come from an area family farm, somehow eating at Dave's and knowing his story of accomplishments against the odds and then how he gave back might be a delicious reminder to pay it forward.

In Hayward, the *Angry Minnow* microbrewery looks a lot like your typical brewpub–burger joint, but this one has a conscience. As its owners the Rasmussen family put it, their operations have "gone green" where sustainability is part of many behind-the-scenes decisions. For instance, the spent grain used in brew production is later used to make Hot and Angry Pretzels and beer bread. And what leftover food hasn't gone bad ends up at a local pig farm. All products are recycled, and some of their dishware is Greenware, which is made from a renewable resin derivative.

## Local Foraging

*Hayward Mercantile Company*, owned by local guy Chef Jeff, is all about Wisconsin, all in one building. On one side is *Truly Wisconsin*, a store that sells regional food and dry goods. On the other is *Truly Delicious Chef Shop*, which sells the kitchenware to go with the cuisine and offers monthly cooking classes and international culinary tours.

In the town of Iron River, one hardly expects to find a place selling Renaissance beverages, but think again. Since 1996, Jon and Kim Hamilton of *White Winter Winery* have been making mead from local honey and fruits, yeast, and water. Taking advantage of the amazing Bayfield County berry and apple production, they are able to source their fruit from nearby farmers who use sustainable growing methods. Bees love all that Bayfield County fruit, and thus the beekeepers who supply the Hamiltons' honey are within a 150-mile radius.

Mead has been around for at least eight thousand years and hasn't changed much during that time. You can sample some in the showroom of their new building on Highway 2. As you sip your honey mead, you'll learn the etymology of the word "honeymoon." It comes from the tradition of giving the newlywed couple a "moon's supply" of mead to ensure a fruitful union. Sweet mead was especially prized for the honeymoon because it was believed that the "sweeter" the mead the more "fruitful" the union. Mead comes in varieties, all made with honey as a base: bracketts are made with added grain, pyments add grapes, melomels add fruit, and metheglins add herbs. The darker the mead, the drier it is. Jon also ferments hard cider.

## What to Do

If you cross-country ski, snowshoe, snow skate, or mountain bike, the *Rock Lake Trail* is less than a half mile from Cable Nature Lodge. Here you'll find five groomed, narrow, classic-only ski trails of varied lengths that cross over rolling to hilly terrain. Some trails involve downhill runs that are long with sharp turns, and some, such as the Rock Lake loop, pass by small lakes, making this a real Northwoods-style skiing experience. Mountain bikers will find several miles of what the Chequamegon Area Mountain Bike Association (CAMBA) describes as "unrelenting hilly terrain" on the Rock Lake Trail. This trail is within a maple and oak forest that includes sporadic stands of large white pines. You can also hike it before the snow falls or strap on snowshoes afterward. This is a good course for getting the heart rate up with its short uphill stints. Hiking on the Rock Lake Trail is best in the short segments between Forest Road 207 and the lakes—Rock Lake, Frels and Hildebrand Lakes, or Spring Lake.

The 1964 Wilderness Act prevents us from spreading our residential neighborhoods and corporate industries over every square inch of the United States, designating certain areas as protected. Good for them and lucky for us. A trip to the Cable area includes ten thousand protected acres within ten miles of town, all still within the *Chequamegon-Nicolet National Forest*. The *Porcupine Lake Wilderness Area* constitutes 4,448 acres of that protected land, offering ample opportunity for silent sports. The *North Country National Scenic Trail*, slated to be the longest connecting trail in the United States (New York to North Dakota), runs an eight-mile path through this rolling oak savannah and its flatland, providing habitat to abundant wildlife, including loons and songbirds. Nonmotorized boaters will find seventy-five-acre Porcupine Lake loaded with bass, pike, and blue-gill, and many trout-stocked streams are nearby.

Farther southeast is another 6,583 acres of protected wilderness at the *Rainbow Lake Wilderness Area*, just four miles north of Drummond. Cross-country skiers and hikers should bring their binoculars to view the timber wolves that are said to pack this territory. Six miles of the North Country National Scenic Trail run through this wilderness area and along remnants of hundred-year-old narrow-gauge logging railways. Birders will not be disappointed with the area's fifteen lakes and nine small ponds, all providing home to nesting and migrating birds and waterfowl.

If you're a canoeist or kayaker looking for rustic and secluded waterways and some good trout fishing, look no further than the *Namekagon River*, the main tributary of the Saint Croix River and a protected part of the Saint Croix National Scenic Riverway. Designated Wild and Scenic by the National Park Service, it shows little development, from its origin in Cable to its end at the Saint Croix River a hundred miles later. Canoeing the Namekagon River promises as primitive a Northwoods experience as it gets. In the little town of Trego, where the Ojibwe once set up open-air campsites, the Namekagon Visitor Center tells river history both on paper and through local storytellers. Here you can meet up with *Jack's Canoe and Tube Rental*, a four-generation family-run outfitter started by Jack Canfield's grandfather in 1935. Jack will rent you a canoe, kayak, or inner tube and then shuttle you up or down the river to designated points. You can camp under the stars like the Ojibwe at one of the primitive, free campsites maintained by the National Park Service.

For a rustic, 99.5-mile-stretch of river and wildlife you can start at Namekagon Lake in the Chequamegon-Nicolet National Forest nine miles east of Cable at the Namekagon Dam (off Dam Road two miles north of County M, close to the CAMBA Telemark Resort Trail Head). Along the thirty-three miles to Hayward, you'll find ten canoe landings, some with access to *National Park Service Campsites*. From Hayward to Trego, a thirty-four-mile stretch and the only "developed" part (that is, homes have been built along the river near Hayward Lake), there are canoe landings at Hayward and Earl Park and eighteen remote campsites. You can camp at Jack's Canoe and Tube Rental (see below for more outfitter information) in Trego, or continue on to Riverside (forty miles), just past the point where the Namekagon River meets the Saint Croix River. Between County K Landing and Riverside Landing, the most isolated stretch of the river with fewer campsites, there are campgrounds at three canoe landings—Riverside, West Howell, and Howell—plus more than thirty primitive campsites. All the sites accommodate groups (up to six tents) and individual campers (up to three tents). These campsites are free, available on a first-come, first-served basis with a three-night maximum stay. For a list of outfitters in the Cable-Trego area, go to www.nps.gov/sacn/planyourvisit/outfitters.htm.

*Down to Earth Tours* begins its seasonal ecotours on Earth Day and runs through October. You can choose from two distinct focuses led by historian and naturalist Dave Thorson: the Eco/Geo/History Tour or the First Americans Cultural Tour. The former explores the Ojibwe traditions and culture and geologic and glacial history of the Chequamegon-Nicolet Forest and its waterways. It's a seven-hour minibus "learning adventure" that traverses one hundred miles, with numerous stops, short hikes, and "a feast in the forest." It leaves from Hayward on Wednesdays and Cable on Fridays. The latter, also a minibus tour that includes a "feast in the forest," explores traditions evident in the land created by Paleo-Indians as far back as ten thousand years, the mound builders, and the Ojibwe who still live in the Northwoods. This tour leaves from Hayward on Saturdays.

Housed in a new space, the *Cable Natural History Museum* continues to promote the appreciation of nature but now it's as green as the land around it. Its extensive education outreach programs continue to target students and teachers in fourteen school districts across northwestern Wisconsin and offer numerous naturalist programs developed for the general public, a lecture series, and field trips throughout the year. But now the staff has a building that's all about clean energy—a geothermal design that takes energy from the earth to heat and cool the facility, double-paned energy efficient windows, passive solar draws, and extensive berming for insulation protection. Museum naturalists will explain the whole alternative energy system. These staffers are understandably proud of this new facility and are enthusiastic about sharing information. Admission is free.

In Spooner the *Wisconsin Canoe Heritage Museum* preserves and restores historic canoes and promotes education about the influence of canoe craft on the art and history of North America. Housed in the historic Baker Grain Elevator (circa 1912), it features a collection of thirty canoes, many from the golden age of North American canoeing and more by contemporary builders. Become a member and you can participate in programs in its state-of-the-art Canoe Shop, a newly renovated space where the museum holds canoe construction and restoration workshops. You can also use the space to build your own canoe.

## Fat-tire Bike the Chequamegon Forest

Mountain bikers, you are well represented in the Cable area by the *Chequamegon Area Mountain Bike Association* (CAMBA), which works hard to promote your rugged but silent sport. CAMBA is a nonprofit mountain bike advocate that promotes education, sustainable trail development, and tourism in the Chequamegon forest area. It practices responsible environmental stewardship by developing trails that will tolerate years of use without degrading land or promoting erosion. In conjunction with the U.S. Forest Service, local governments and agencies, and private land owners, CAMBA manages over three hundred miles of marked and mapped mountain bike trail clusters in near-wildness areas in the towns of Cable, Delta, Drummond, Hayward, Namekagon, and Seely. Its website describes eight trail clusters throughout the Cable area and offers a map of all the CAMBA trails in the Chequamegon forest area. These trails run through national and county forests and private land.

Alan Craig, the museum's curator and legacy consultant for the Sigurd Olson Environmental Institute, says he will add to the collection and develop its programming each year. Past exhibits have included Canoes of Wisconsin and an exhibit dedicated to Sigurd Olson, one of the most influential conservationists of the twentieth century.

### Local Arts

*Sara Qualey*'s paintings are as lush as the produce she brings home from the farmers' market: cage-free eggs, organic purple turnips, bright orange pumpkins. You can visit her studio on Blue Moon Road in Cable where you'll find her as welcoming and warm as the palette of oils she uses to reproduce what she calls "the simple things in everyday life." She's a member of North Star Homestead Farms CSA, and says that she always returns from the market ready to paint whatever is in season. She is one of the four Blue Moon Road Artists who open their studios for an art tour every September. But you can also visit her studio by appointment.

*Mulberry Street* is a home decor and vintage store halfway between Cable and Hayward with an espresso bar and microbrews. This place is jammed with high-end vintage items and antiques at low-end prices. It also features quality local art, like Sara Qualey's wonderful oil paintings.

*Annual Events*

Thousands of mountain bikers flock to Cable in September for the annual *Chequamegon Fat Tire Festival*. The main event, the Chequamegon 40, is a forty-mile, mass-start event that begins in downtown Hayward and ends in Cable. It travels over the American Birkebeiner cross-country ski trails, forest roads, and other wooded trails. But there are events for varied abilities and durabilities, like the Short and Fat, designed for new off-road bikers, younger riders, and nonmarathoners. The Chequamegon Fat Tire Festival website (www.cheqfattire.com) has all the specifics, including the event that is best geared for your ability.

The *American Birkebeiner* is a world-class cross-country ski race patterned after the Birkebeiner Rennet, a re-creation of a thirteenth-century event in Norway when warrior soldiers (Birkebeiners), named for their birchbark leggings, skied Prince Haakon to safety during the Norwegian civil war. Rigorous by its very nature, it brings skiers from around the world to compete and can fairly claim to promote a healthy lifestyle. Its website (www.birkie.com) has loads of information on the event and how to train.

---

### Lifelong Learning in the Northwoods

The *Telemark Educational Foundation* people call themselves a "Northwoods Interactive Resource Center that is designed to enhance lifelong learning." Go to their website (www.telemarkeducation.com) and you'll see why. This foundation offers a huge range of enrichment classes, from quilting retreats to belly dancing to a Growing Green program that garners appreciation for native plants and wildlife and just getting your and your kids' hands in the dirt.

---

# Far from the Madding Crowds

## Chetek and New Auburn Area

In Wildness is the preservation of the World.

—Henry David Thoreau, "Walking" (1862)

Barron County seems to be one of those places that missed being the homecoming queen by a vote. The little town of Chetek (*sheetak* is Ojibwe for pelican or swan) is slow paced, claiming six lakes and a multitude of resorts along 120 acres of shoreline. While you'll hear the locals call this the Northwoods, it lacks the showy roadside display of towering white and red pines and the contrasting grays of Wisconsin birches. But crowded people- and car-filled streets don't exist. And it is home to one of Wisconsin's premier resorts, debatably *the* premier resort, where sustainable practices are so imbedded in their operations they might not think to mention it.

In New Auburn, a short jog southeast from Chetek, where a rolling, wooded terrain kicks the landscape up a notch, is a bed-and-breakfast that runs on more renewable energy options than arguably any lodge in the state. A stay might keep you from getting in your car for the duration, but if you're antsy to explore the area you can hike the gentle hills of the Chippewa County leg of the Ice Age Trail or bike along its shallow kettles or forge a variegated landscape on cross-country skis. You can also hire an outfitter that has the edge on ecotours in the state. You'll learn about indigenous plants and wetlands, or simply paddle the Chippewa Moraine's numerous waterways . . . it's your call.

## Where to Stay

*Canoe Bay* in Chetek is one classy eco-act. This all-inclusive getaway set in hilly, lake-laden terrain at the edge of the Chippewa Moraine Unit in Barron County is simple, elegant, serene, and sincere. If you don't ask if your meals are made up of all organically and locally grown and raised ingredients, you might never know that they are. Loudly advertising their earth-sustaining policies is not part of Canoe Bay's sophistication. To provide the best with the lowest carbon footprint is just part of owners Lisa and Dan Dobrowolski's personal philosophy and style of hospitality. They wouldn't think of doing it any other way.

If you are unfamiliar with John Rattenbury of the Taliesin architects and the Frank Lloyd Wright School of Architecture when you arrive, you might feel schooled in his organic style by the time you check out. Rattenbury's signature designs—abstract cut-glass windows, clean and arched structural lines, passive energy–gathering window placements—run throughout the resort alongside other Wright-inspired buildings. Two units, the Rattenbury Cottage and the Edgewood Villa, were designed by Rattenbury on-site (others were designed by Kelly Davis of SALA Architects in Minneapolis). And they are nothing short of exquisite, a term not commonly used to describe lodging in Wisconsin's Northwoods. Other lodging options consist of cottages and inn-style rooms. These units combine the earth-driven lines of these Wisconsin native sons with the wooded, kettled landscape of this lower northwestern region. Both are inescapable, as the buildings are perched, unassumingly, against the natural horizon line of a secluded lake setting.

You won't see Canoe Bay on the Travel Green Wisconsin website any time soon, according to Lisa, because she and Dan are "fiercely independent." And they probably don't need the publicity. Canoe Bay is the only Relais and Chateaux lodging member in the Midwest, speaking to the rare availability of its level of luxury, far superior to most accommodations found in this neck of the woods—or most of the Northwoods for that matter. Yet there is no reason to be intimidated by its upscale presence. The Dobrowolskis are very friendly, as is their staff. The entrenched sustainable practices that make Canoe Bay one of Wisconsin's greener travel choices come from the owners' homage to responsible land stewardship, a mindset passed down from Dan's grandparents, who were farmers just north of Canoe Bay's 280-acre compound, where he vacationed as a boy. What he and Lisa brought to the venture was an intelligent approach to

The John Rattenbury–designed cottages at Canoe Bay in Chetek are built to blend with the natural landscape and overlook one of three lakes on the Canoe Bay property. (photo courtesy of Canoe Bay)

design and their enormous respect for the soil on which they have built this sustainable beauty.

But to call Canoe Bay "green" would understate its purpose. Their ecology-minded policies are much more a way of life than any recent trend to stave off further effects of global warming. They are solidly committed to maintaining the trio of DNR-rated pristine lakes they inherited with the property (no personal lake equipment allowed, but canoes and kayaks are available for use) and to forging personal relationships with local organic farmers who grow produce and meat specifically for their remarkable Canoe Bay cuisine. And they use few synthetic products.

The Dobrowolskis have left no stone unturned in renovating the property's original buildings and new structures to provide luxury, relaxation, and a dining experience with every sustainable means available. Their gardener, John, keeps the grounds rich with earth-sustaining native wildflowers and grasses, many of which appear indoors in summer, artfully arranged by an on-site florist. John is also the steward of the inn's three-acre organic garden whose daily harvest ends up on the menu.

Despite the fact that you won't find a nonorganic ingredient on Canoe Bay's top-notch seasonal dinner menu, or that its buildings are designed from the ground up to maximize passive solar energy, the Dobrowolskis are low key about how green they really are—perhaps because they are to the core. They are located near Chetek, not far from Highway 53. Directions are provided for first-time guests so they don't get lost.

Farther southeast, nestled in the Chippewa Valley near the Blue Diamond Recreation Area, Kathy Duffy and Steve Krug run a B&B whose energy is sealed up as tightly as a steel drum. *Jacks Lake Bed and Breakfast* in New Auburn is a clean, charming hostelry that's without a doubt the go-to place for anyone interested in learning about renewable energy sources. Steve recently sold his renewable energy business, which had made this off-grid home, their second since the 1970s, a veritable testing ground. Now running it as a bed-and-breakfast on the shores of Jacks Lake, Kathy and Steve allow guests to simply enjoy the rural surroundings or, for a fee, get consultation on renewable energy. The sources of most of this B&B's energy are examples of what works best. With a wind turbine, solar panels, photovoltaic panels, and an outdoor wood-burning stove supplying hot water in winter months when the sun is scarce, these guys are hooked up. Kathy will tell you that before you raise a wind turbine or invest in solar panels, do the small stuff: insulate, pull the plug on the constant energy draws in your house, like the

A wind turbine is just one clean energy option at Jacks Lake Bed and Breakfast in New Auburn. Guests can get a tutorial on the many ways this lodge runs energy entirely off the grid. (photo courtesy of Jacks Lake Bed and Breakfast)

computer and clock radios and cable television box. That's a free tidbit. She's full of very friendly free advice. Kathy's breakfasts are traditional and as sustainable as her local markets will allow.

Amenities include a hot tub, a sauna, plush terrycloth robes, and private bathrooms. Two of the accommodations are suites. A deck overlooks Jacks Lake and Kathy's perennial flower gardens. You can lounge on a small sand beach or a dock, or float on a raft or in a canoe. Kathy and Steve provide a volleyball and badminton court and bocce balls. The entire place is wholesome and enlightening with loads of clean and free energy.

### Where to Eat

The Rice Lake area isn't jam packed with sustainable table options, but the *Adventures Restaurant and Pub* owners hail from Minneapolis and have brought one to town. The Goode family had enough of the Twin Cities rat race, packed their bags, and moved to Rice Lake and opened Adventures

Restaurant and Pub where they practice their "earth-friendly, corporate citizen" ethic. On the menu you'll find all kinds of local ingredients, like cheese from the Burnett Dairy in Alpha and grass-fed beef from the On Twin Lakes Store and Family Farm (see Local Foraging), along with elk from Cannon Falls, Minnesota. They're staunch recyclers and use their location as a drop-off site for household batteries.

## Local Foraging

*On Twin Lakes Store and Family Farm* in Birchwood, thirty-seven miles north of Chetek, is more than the Brunclik family farm. The pride they have in what they do is shared with anyone who wants to see how humanely they raise their grass-fed cattle and homegrown-vegetable-fed pigs. On their three hundred acres you may hike, ski, or take your horse along the farm's marked trail system that skirts its woods, fields, gardens, and pumpkin patches. They have wagon rides in summer and sleigh rides in winter for family or group outings. And while in the area, baseball fans can support the local Brill Millers (www.leaguelineup.com/brillbaseball), an Independent League baseball team in Birchwood on which Brunclik family members have been playing for generations.

When you can pick your own chemical-free apples in autumn at a price that's competitive with conventionally grown apples, it's worth the twenty-nine-mile trip from either Chetek or New Auburn. In the little town of Turtle Lake, east of Chetek, Ken Mandley of *Deedon Lake Natural Orchard* grows chemical-free apples with concern for long-term soil health. He minimizes soil compaction by allowing orchard floor clippings to naturally compost into the soil. Mandley says he provides a local organic fruit option while significantly reducing harmful environmental impacts caused by modern shipment and storage of fruit, pointing out that most organic fruit in stores is shipped from California, Washington, Chile, and New Zealand. Plus, he provides a healthful fruit at a reasonable cost—U-Pick costs about a dollar a pound, about a third to a half of the cost of organic apples in stores and about the same or slightly less than conventionally grown apples. Worth the trip? You bet!

Randy Lee is a jack-of-all-trades. He studied nuclear physics in college but ended up a computer geek. And when he's not playing the Hardanger fiddle in church, he's running a brewery with his wife, Ann, in Dallas, just eleven miles southwest of Chetek. Their *Viking Brewing Company* uses sustainable brewing practices—no chemicals, preservatives, or clarifying

### Help Maintain the Ice Age Trail

The Ice Age Trail Management advises: "On all trail segments, make sure you carry a good supply of water, and wear good footwear. Plan your hikes carefully, to ensure enough time. If you camp overnight, make sure you are not camping on private land. Respect the private landowner's rights."

agents are used—and each batch gets its own yeast, unlike some breweries that reuse it. The twenty-two varieties, five of which are available year-round, are natural, unpasteurized, and sterile filtered. Randy and Ann brew their beer in a historic creamery building and invite you to Dallas for a tour on Saturdays. Call ahead; sometimes Randy and Ann are at beer shows.

## What to Do

Less than a mile down Highway 40 from Jacks Lake in New Auburn, herbalist Gigi Stafne runs *Mi Zi Zak Kayaks*, an outfitter that conducts plant and paddling eco-tours on the Ice Age lakes and the Chippewa, Thornapple, Red Cedar, and Flambeau rivers. Gigi leads "nature as healing" tours, mind and body events, yoga on Jacks Lake, as well as camping along the Ice Age Trail for groups, families, organizations, and individuals. And that's just some of what Gigi and her crew do. They also hold kayak and safety camps and a whole battery of nature driven excursions and eco-tours.

The six-mile segment of the Ice Age Trail in the Chippewa Moraine Unit of the Ice Age National Scientific Reserve is thought to be the most scenic in the state. The trail moves with a gentler sweep, or "dead ice" moraines, than the hilly terrain found in southeastern Wisconsin's Kettle Moraine Unit. As a result, the kettles are shallow and the area is great for hiking. The trail is ungroomed but can also be used for snowshoeing and some cross-country skiing. It begins at Plummer Lake and extends westward to Shattuck Lake and County Road M just east of New Auburn. Visit the *Ice Age Interpretive Center* at the *Chippewa Moraine State Recreation Area* to learn about the Ice Age Trail through interactive stations and windows that illustrate Ice Age terminology. The area has over three thousand acres of prairie, wetland, and kettle lakes. You can bike there from Chetek but it's on-road biking. From Chetek take County Road D east to Highway 40 south, to 152nd Street

(Sand Lake Road) south, to County Road M west to the Chippewa Moraine State Recreation Area.

*Blue Hills Trail*, a twenty-three-mile cross-country trail system in northern Rusk County, is twenty-six miles north of Chetek just outside the town of Bruce. The trails traverse a rolling terrain within a largely deciduous forest not without its stands of pine. With small streams that rise and fall with this undulating landscape, it's not only beautiful northern territory, but can present as easy or as challenging a cross-country run as skiers are up for. In snowless months these trails are used by mountain bikers, but they were developed for skiers by skiers. There's a charming log warming house. The east side of the trail system is for non-motorized use but hikers and bikers will find the west side the most user-friendly. The trailhead is located on the east side of Fire Lane Road, 2.5 miles north of the road's intersection with County Road O just off Highway 40. For a list of more Rusk County Trail Systems go to www.ruskcountywi.com/recreation.hike-birdwatch.php.

# Spiritual Getaway

## Clark County Forest Area

Saint Francis is the patron saint of ecology and peacemaking.

— Christine Center

On a quiet country road in western Clark County, along the eastern edge of miles and miles of forest, you'll find the remote but internationally known Christine Center. (Use the directions the center gives you; Google maps has no idea where the place is.) This peaceful retreat, founded in 1980 by Franciscan Sister Mary Barta and rooted in the Catholic mystical tradition, welcomes people of all spiritual paths without proselytizing. According to Sister Johanna Seubert, a common ground of those who go there is often simply the desire for harmony with the earth—a central tenet of the Franciscan order—and a contemplative life. Daily morning yoga and meditation in the Gathering Room, wooded trails to explore, massage services, a wood-fired sauna, comfortable lodging, delicious vegetarian fare, peace and quiet: all add up to a lovely respite for a weekend or longer. And it's not just for those seeking solitude; the sisters welcome families with children and groups planning a retreat.

From the beginning, it's been an earth-friendly place. The center was originally housed in a recycled barn with a silo chapel. Today's center was built with reused and natural materials, many harvested locally, with the silo as entry room and bell tower. In recent years, they've added a solar-powered outbuilding and converted the main building to geothermal heating and cooling.

On one of the Christine Center's hiking trails, an ecumenical shrine made with found materials reflects the center's guiding principles of environmental conservation and openness to all faiths. (photo by Robert Diebel)

A solar array heats the water in the Christine Center's Siloe Building, where guests can do laundry and campers can take showers. (photo by Robert Diebel)

Roald Gundersen's Whole Trees Architecture and Construction works on the Kara Woods Residence at the Christine Center. (photo by Robert Diebel)

An outlying "Whole Tree House," where two Franciscan sisters who recently joined the community live, was built with an innovative approach created by Roald Gundersen of Whole Trees Architecture and Construction (www.wholetreesarchitecture.com) in Stoddard. Permaculture techniques are reconfiguring the center's vegetable plots. During shared meals in the dining hall, guests are often drawn into fascinating conversations about sustainability.

### Getting There

The Christine Center is twenty-five quiet country miles from the Stanley Travel Stop on the *Jefferson* bus line between Milwaukee and Minneapolis which has connections to Madison and Chicago.

### Where to Stay

Lodging at the *Christine Center* ranges from the rustic to the modern. A campground and the Hermitages—fifteen cabins constructed over the past thirty years in a delightful variety of quirky building styles and graced with names like Gabriel, Uriel, and Guadalupe—are scattered throughout the forested grounds. The cabins accommodate from one to five people. Those known as Rustic Hermitages have electricity, woodstoves for heat, water nearby, and outhouses rather than indoor plumbing. Campers and Rustic Hermitage guests can use the bathrooms and showers in the solar-powered Siloe building; there's also a laundry in that building. Modern Hermitages each have thermostatically controlled heat, bathrooms with shower, and well-outfitted kitchenettes. The Guest House rooms, located in a wing of the main building, each provide space for two people, a private bath, maximum peace and quiet, and close proximity to the dining hall, library, and Gathering Room.

### Where to Eat

Meals at the Christine Center, hearty and totally delicious vegetarian feasts often made from ingredients grown at the center or locally, are served buffet style. Guests may sign up for individual meals or three meals a day. Small tables make solitary dining possible, though many guests gather around the large tables for the chance to meet others. Cloth napkins in a basket, personalized with rings, add a green and friendly touch. Even if you cook your own meals in your cabin, you should eat at least once in the dining room.

Ingredients for the vegetarian fare served at the Christine Center come in part from the center's organic garden, where gardeners practice permaculture methods. (photo by Robert Diebel)

## Local Foraging

If you choose a Hermitage with a kitchenette, you can cook with locally raised foods. From June to October, you'll find local fruit and produce, meats, cheeses, baked goods, and other products at nearby farmers' markets: by the Kwik Trip in Loyal on Tuesday afternoons and Saturday mornings; on State Highway 73 in Greenwood on Wednesday afternoons; and in Neillsville's Town Square on Saturday mornings.

Five miles north of the center, *North Hendren Co-op Dairy*, in operation since 1923, has been producing Black River gorgonzola and blue cheese since 2001. Both cheeses are first place winners in recent United States Championship Cheese Contests, and the gorgonzola won a first place/grand master award at the World Dairy Expo in 2003. You can buy these tasty prize winners and the dairy's other cheeses at the co-op store, but call ahead to be sure it's open. The dairy is a nonprofit cooperative owned by local farmers, and the milk is local, fresh, and farmer-certified rBGH free.

Speaking of cheese, northwestern Clark County is home to another prize-winning artisan cheese. Marieke Gouda, an aged farmstead gouda crafted by the Penterman family just east of Thorp, is made with milk from their own herd. Rolf and Marieke Penterman are first-generation Wisconsin dairy farmers who came to Clark County from the Netherlands, where Marieke learned to make authentic Dutch gouda. In 2007, after only six months of cheesemaking in Clark County, Marieke's Gouda Foenegreek took Best of Class for flavored semisoft cheeses in the United States Championship Cheese Contest. Since then, her goudas have won about thirty more national and international awards. You can buy Marieke's gouda on the farm at *Holland's Family Cheese* retail store, about twenty miles north of the Christine Center, or look online for other retail outlets. Please call ahead for creamery tours.

## What to Do

The Christine Center's year-round series of workshops and seminars covers topics on yoga, meditation, gardening, writing, and spirituality, with natural themes interwoven, as in the fall "Women's Equinox Retreat."

If you're not there for a workshop, you can do morning yoga in the Gathering Room, hike or cross-country ski on the center's 120 acres, and steam in the sauna. Make an appointment with Roberta Hodges for an Ananda massage session at the Mary Sophia Hermitage across from the campground, or for Myofascial Therapy at Villa de Plenty across from the Basil Hermitage.

Voluntourism, a work exchange program, is another reason people come to the Christine Center, where one simply exchanges thirty-five hours a week of center work for room and board, leaving plenty of free time.

Those who want to venture beyond can bicycle on lightly traveled roads to swimming beaches and hiking trails at nearby *Mead Lake County Park* and *Rock Dam County Park*, deep in the county forest land. The Clark County forest, created in 1934 to rescue land abandoned by strip logging and failed homesteads, is now sustainably managed for lumber and recreation (see Certifying a Forest).

ATV and snowmobile trails are common in many parts of the forest, so for a quieter experience, head fifteen miles south to Neillsville. At the *Levis/Trow Mound Recreation Area* just southwest of Neillsville, thirty-four miles of nonmotorized county forest trails are reserved for mountain biking, hiking, cross-country skiing, and snowshoeing. The often steep trails circle

A volunteer carries trim strips he cut to finish the interior of the Christine Center's new green-built addition. (photo by Robert Diebel)

and ascend the Levis and Trow Mounds (monadnocks, or isolated rock mounds found on the fringe of the Driftless Area). Experienced mountain bikers say the trails are exceptionally well designed.

*The Highground*, a Wisconsin Vietnam Veterans Memorial Project in Neillsville, has four miles of walking trails and holds an annual biking fundraiser, with rides ranging from 147 to 466 miles.

The Black River bisects Clark County, and white-water enthusiasts can enjoy paddling a nice stretch of Class 2 rapids downstream of Neillsville, a day trip described in Mike Svob's *Paddling Northern Wisconsin*.

## Certifying a Forest

The Clark County Forest covers 133,000 acres of the ecological province called eastern broadleaf forest. This public land is certified by the Forest Stewardship Council (FSC). When we talked with the Wisconsin DNR about certification, Rebecca Gass of the Forestry Division said, "This is a big deal. Wisconsin, Minnesota, and Michigan together have the largest acreage of third-party-certified forests in the nation. Being certified is like the process a farm has to go through to be organic—you need to prove that you're managing the land sustainably, which includes social and economic standards. They have to be audited every year, with a complete reevaluation every three years. Wisconsin's county forests are pretty cool, really the forest workhorses in the state. More recreation and timber management happens there than in any other public land, state and national combined."

Modern forest management includes new challenges like battling invasive species, controlling tree diseases that result from fire suppression, minimizing forest fragmentation caused by new development, and resolving mixed-use conflicts in fair ways that also preserve the overall health of the forest. You can read fascinating and detailed FSC certification reports (118 pages in 2009) at the DNR's website (http://dnr.wi.gov/forestry/county/countyForestCert.htm). There's a financial piece as well, about a rising consumer demand for certified forest products that can yield local economic growth. FSC certification is one of the two most widely accepted forest certification systems in North America. Wisconsin's twenty-seven certified county forests cover more than 1.46 million acres, the largest public landholding in the state. This land is in the public trust, and forest certification is part of upholding that trust. We agree that this is a big deal.

# Earth-Friendly Retreat

## Lake Pepin Area

May the countryside and the gliding valley streams content me. Lost to fame, let me love river and woodland.

— VIRGIL, *Eclogues*

For several hundred years, Lake Pepin has lured travelers with its spectacular natural beauty. Just to clarify, it's not a true lake, but a reach of the Mississippi where the river widens behind a natural dam. As the last glacier melted, the strong flow of Wisconsin's Chippewa River dumped enormous amounts of sediment into the more sluggish Mississippi at their confluence. The sediment formed a delta that backed up the big river into what looks like a big lake. Cradled between the grand, craggy bluffs of the Mississippi valley, Lake Pepin has more than its share of spectacular geography.

Quiet roads winding up the bluffs invite bicyclists. Three State Natural Areas draw nature lovers. In spring and fall, birders know the valley as the Mississippi Flyway, prime territory for witnessing the winged migration of bald eagles, tundra swans, egrets, and all their friends. Hikers tramp trails through the wooded coulees (narrow valleys) and up the bluffs for the breathtaking views. (The first explorers, gazing upward from river level, thought the lines of bluffs four hundred feet high were mountain ranges.) And the lake is ever popular with sailing boats.

Local architectural history is alive and well: in the villages of Maiden Rock and Stockholm, rows of restored period buildings are squeezed between the river and the steep bluffs. A lively arts community sponsors events like the summer Stockholm Art Fair and the Fresh Art spring and fall tours. The area's sustainable agriculture scene is booming.

In winter, snowshoe the bluffs. The rugged landscape has the black and white beauty of a woodcut or etching, a beauty even greater than lush green, which obscures rather than reveals. Each tree on the heavily forested bluffs is highlighted in snow, and rounded hills are outlined by dark shaded coulees. Below—the wide, white, frozen expanse of Lake Pepin.

Add lodging and spa services at a peaceful eco-retreat, eateries serving delicious sustainably grown food, and you have the recipe for the tastiest of getaways.

### Getting There

Maiden Rock is fifteen miles from Red Wing, Minnesota, and fifty miles from Winona, Minnesota, which are both on the *Amtrak* Empire Builder route—Chicago to Minneapolis and on to the West Coast. If you board at a station with checked baggage hours (check online) and get off at Winona, Amtrak allows bikes to be checked as baggage in a box, for a fee.

### Where to Stay

In a quiet coulee carved by the Little Rush River, three miles from the village of Maiden Rock, nestles the *Journey Inn*. And indeed, this retreat offers guests the chance for a journey inward. The inn is tucked cozily into the naturally protective features of the coulee. The high steep slope of Morgan Coulee Goat Prairie rises like a shield on the north, its grass-covered face broken by limestone outcrops and clusters of gnarled old oaks. To the south the land slopes down through the inn's restored prairie to woods along the spring-fed creek.

"We came to the Lake Pepin community to create a 'space' for ourselves and others," said Charlene Torchia, proprietor. "Our guests come for the peace and quiet they find here," added John Huffaker, her husband and co-proprietor.

Using green building materials and techniques, the pair built their inn to be as healthful for the earth as it is for humans. In summer, cross-ventilation and ceiling fans—and backup air-conditioning for super-humid days—keep things cool. In winter, floors are warmed from beneath by what Charlene and John call a "solar sandbox," heated by a solar hot water system. Passive solar design, an energy-efficient boiler, and a classic soapstone wood-burning

Solar panels help heat the green-built Journey Inn near Maiden Rock. (photo by Robert Diebel)

stove radiating in the commons heat the space as well. A solar collector provides hot water. An air-exchange system provides continuous fresh ventilation year-round. They use natural cleaning products, soaps, and scents.

The large sunny room at the building's center feels like a cozy, inviting home. Eclectic decor makes it both attractive and comfortable. The proprietors' living quarters and the kitchen are out of sight at one end of the building. At the other end of the common room are four equally appealing guest rooms, each with private bath and either a patio or deck.

Using VOC-free clay and earth plasters and paints, Charlene finished each room herself to reflect one of the four elements—earth, air, water, and fire. Decor is local artwork. The beds have mattresses of natural latex wrapped in wool and organic cotton. Organic cotton, wool, and bamboo bedding completes the eco-comfort quotient.

A vacation rental for families and groups is available in the *Cottage at Journey Inn*, a separate building with its own fully equipped kitchen, living area with wood-burning stove, two bedrooms, and two bathrooms.

And then there's the food. "It started with food," said Charlene, "In the early seventies, I moved from Pennsylvania to Minneapolis for the great

### Curried Apple Squash Soup

*2 tablespoons organic butter
*1 medium onion, chopped
*1 (1 $\frac{1}{2}$ pound) butternut squash, peeled, seeded, and thinly sliced
$\frac{1}{2}$ tablespoon curry powder
*1 large apple, peeled, cored, and chopped
*2 $\frac{1}{2}$ cups chicken or vegetable broth
dash of sherry or brandy
* $\frac{1}{2}$ cup organic half-and-half
$\frac{1}{2}$ tablespoon Worcestershire sauce (optional, vegetarian)
sea salt and freshly ground pepper, to taste.

Melt butter in a two-quart saucepan or soup pot and sauté onion and squash for twenty minutes. Add apples and continue to sauté until softened. Add stock, bring to boil, then reduce to simmer. Add sherry. When squash is very soft, turn off heat. Use an immersion blender to puree soup. Add half-and-half as you puree. Add Worcestershire sauce, salt, and pepper.

—Charlene Torchia, Journey Inn

*Local ingredient

food co-ops, and now the local and organic food scene around here is amazing." Her cooking reflects both her passion for sustainable local food and her roots in the Calabrian Italian food traditions of her childhood. B&B guests are served a full brunch on weekends and a hearty, healthful breakfast on weekdays. Charlene's meals make you want to sing (in Italian, of course).

Speaking of food—

### Where to Eat

In the tiny village of Maiden Rock (pop. 130), Sandra Thielman at the *Smiling Pelican Bake Shop* offers her desserts, artisan breads, quiches, muffins, cookies, and pies. Her trademark: lavender-ginger cookies.

### Journey Inn Frittata

\* | medium onion, chopped
| tablespoon olive oil
\*2 cloves garlic
\*6–8 leaves of organic kale or chard, chopped (chop stems in small pieces and
    add with the garlic)
\*8 large free-range eggs
\* $^1/_2$–| cup of organic asiago or parmesan cheese, grated (from the Eau Galle
    Cheese Factory)
sea salt and freshly ground pepper to taste
Optional additions: mushrooms, | tablespoon of red wine vinegar, herbs, other
    cheeses

Heat a cast iron frying pan. Add olive oil and sauté onions on low heat till
soft and carmelized. Mince garlic and add with chopped stems. Put on lid and
simmer. Add chopped greens. Stir until greens are mixed in, cover, and let wilt.
Beat eggs, and add salt, pepper, and cheese. Add mixture to veggies. Don't
stir. Cook on low heat with lid on pan. When eggs begin to set, run a spatula
around the edges of the pan and make a cross in the center. To finish, place pan
under oven broiler for five minutes to cook top. Serves 4–6.

—Charlene Torchia, Journey Inn

\*Local ingredient

Six miles south in teeny tiny Stockholm (pop. 97), the *Bogus Creek
Cafe and Bakery* offers both indoor seating and a garden patio for breakfast
and lunch. Local and regional ingredients include lots of seasonal produce,
Organic Valley mozzarella, Grassland cheddar, Winona flour, locally brewed
Rush River Beer on tap, and Wollersheim wines. Huettl's Locker in Lake
City supplies custom-cured smoked bacon and sausage. A gluten-free
menu is available. Owner Colleen Flynn also bakes and sells artisan breads
like Wisconsin cheddar, cranberry walnut, and cinnamon-raisin. A big green
plus: Colleen recycles everything, including food waste. "Rather than

For a truly local eating experience, ask Charlene and John at the Journey Inn about Tuesday pizza at A to Z Produce and Bakery. (photo by Robert Diebel)

disposing of organic waste into a dumpster, I collect it throughout the day and donate it to a local farmer. The chickens and goats receive a well-rounded, nutritional diet, and I don't clutter my dumpster with nutritionally rich waste. Once in a while, I am lucky enough to get an organically raised, delicious, plump chicken in return. It's a win-win situation. You would laugh to see the chickens *running* when their treats are delivered!" she said.

Across the street, Janet Garretson of the *Stockholm Pie Company* serves handmade pies and other desserts made with fresh ingredients, including local blueberries and Wisconsin apples. Other local ingredients include maple syrup from Weiss Woods of Plum Creek (www.weisswoods.com) and ice cream from Timm's Dairy in Eau Claire.

For an outdoor eating adventure, ask Charlene and John at Journey Inn about Tuesday pizza on the farm at *A to Z Produce and Bakery.* Totally local, totally delicious.

## Local Foraging

On the bluffs above the Mississippi, sustainable agriculture is growing strong. Harvest some of that local goodness to carry home. At *Rush River Produce*, pick your own red, black, and white currants, gooseberries, fall raspberries, and blueberries—thirteen different varieties—all raised by the Cuddy family using sustainable methods. They also sell their garden produce and locally produced honey and maple syrup. Views from the bluff-top farm are inspiring.

Pick your own at *Maiden Rock Orchard*, choosing from twenty-five apple varieties, including heirlooms and crab apples (which make a lovely jelly). In addition to this biodiversity, owners Herdie Baisden and Carol Wiersma use organic methods and integrated pest management (IPM) to minimize spraying. Their IPM approach involves raptor perches, owl nesting boxes, bat houses, and bumblebee houses to encourage natural predators. Flowers and other plantings attract helpful insects. Call ahead for hours and directions.

If you're not into fruit picking, buy their apples, hard cider, and fruit wines at the orchard or in Stockholm at *Stockholm General*, formerly known as the Good Apple. Renamed by owner Steven Grams, it focuses on local and Wisconsin products. In addition to Maiden Rock apples and products like Grandaddy's Apple 2-Pepper Chutney, they carry Wisconsin craft beers, wines, and cheeses, including Blaser's Cheese from Comstock.

*Honey Hill Apiary*, in the hills above Maiden Rock, sells local honey and beeswax candles. Call ahead for hours and directions.

Charlene Torchia of Journey Inn buys her organic, pasture-raised meats from *Anderson's Farm* near Arkansaw. And while she's in that area, she buys her certified organic parmesan and asiago cheese from the *Eau Galle Cheese Factory* just north of Durand, owned and operated by the Buhlman family since 1945. The Eau Galle retail store is open daily, and you can tour the factory while you're there to see these excellent cheeses being made.

On their *Blue Gentian Farm* east of New Richmond, Darryle and Renee Powers use sustainable agriculture methods to raise heirloom livestock breeds of beef, lamb, pork, turkey, and chicken, as well as heirloom vegetables and eggs from Black Australorp chickens. They sell vegetables and retail cuts of their meats at their farm store (open daily) and welcome visitors. It's forty-eight miles from Maiden Rock—a bit of a hike—so bring a picnic and explore the farm's hundred acres of restored tall grass prairie while you're there.

## What to Do

Things to do without ever leaving the Journey Inn's sixty-six acres: Hike or snowshoe on trails through the prairie, down to the creek, and up to the ridge. Meditate in the Labyrinth. Lounge in a hammock by the creek. Sit by the woodstove and read.

The Journey Inn is also a spa and learning center. Charlene and other licensed massage practitioners offer individual massage, couples massage, or a whole spa day. John, a licensed psychotherapist and a life direction coach, does consultations at the inn. Journey Inn also hosts women's spa retreats, Artist's Way workshops, writer's weekend retreats, seasonal retreats, silent retreat weekends, Enneagram workshops for couples, and other events. Their website and e-newsletter list current offerings.

The Journey Inn hosts the *Lake Pepin Farm and Food Tour*, which combines a stay at the inn, brunches and snacks, a tasty farm tour of local food producers, and a local foods cooking class with Linda Harding of *The Kitchen Sage*.

Take a cooking class focused on local ingredients with chef Judy Krohn, formerly of the Harbor View Cafe in Pepin and now house chef at *The Palate*, a gourmet kitchen store in Stockholm.

Kayakers and canoeists who want to paddle Lake Pepin will find a boat launch in the Maiden Rock Village Park.

## Out-of-State Adventures

Bicycle thirteen miles north of Maiden Rock on the Great River Road and cross the Mississippi on Highway 63 into the historic river town of Red Wing, Minnesota. Just over the bridge, Barn Bluff Park has good (and often steep) hiking trails and great views of the Mississippi River valley. The west-facing slope of Barn Bluff is a large goat prairie (a dry, tall-grass, hill prairie, common in the upper Mississippi River valley), covered in early spring with a vast Pasque flower bloom, a carpet of purple. A trail map with directions to the main access is online at www.livehealthyredwing.org (this impressive website has maps of all Red Wing biking and hiking trails). If it's a weekend, try lunch at Sarah's (www.sarahsinredwing.com), an independent restaurant at 307 Main Street in Red Wing. There's more. On the west side of Red Wing, you can access the Cannon Valley Trail (www.cannonvalleytrail.com), a 19.7 mile rail trail up the gorgeous Cannon River Valley.

Bicycle the bluffs on a network of quiet byways through scenic farmland. You can ride the Great River Road (Highway 35), although traffic can be vexing on busy weekends. There's a quieter nine-mile loop along the Rush River valley. From the Great River Road, head north on County Road A. Turn right at 385th Street to return south to the Great River Road.

*Morgan Coulee Prairie State Natural Area*, just across the road from the inn, is one of the last large-scale dry prairies left in this part of the state. Hike up the bluff for great views.

Hike or snowshoe four-hundred-foot *Maiden Rock Bluff State Natural Area* to see prairie and oak savannah restoration. Two established trails—one wooded, the other prairie—offer about a mile of easy hiking and a spectacular view of the river valley, especially grand when dressed in fall colors. Peregrine falcons nest on the rocky bluff; banding of chicks is done each year in the preserve. The bluff, 2.5 miles northwest of Stockholm, is also habitat for gyrfalcon, golden eagle, bald eagle, and turkey vulture. Please stay on the trails to avoid the sensitive natural areas.

*Rush River Delta State Natural Area* is a floodplain forest at the mouth of the Rush River, west of Maiden Rock on Highway 35 at the intersection with County A. Look for Forster's tern, common tern, red-shouldered hawk,

Acadian flycatcher, cerulean warbler, and prothonotary warbler. The preserve contains a small great blue heron rookery.

*Local Arts*

Shop the eclectic *Abode Gallery* in Stockholm. You'll find original fine art by local artists, custom Abode private label furniture handcrafted by regional artisans, and other furnishings by local and Wisconsin artists.

Stockholm is full of interesting shops and galleries. Paul Taylor's *Northern Oak Amish Furniture* and Diane Millner's *Stockholm Pottery and Mercantile* are two that carry locally produced items.

In a repurposed harness shop, Paul and Pam Larson's indie bookstore, *A Sense of Place*, has a great selection of illustrated children's books on nature, an impressive array of nature guidebooks, and books on environmentalism and regional history. They also carry discovery items for kids, such as bug kits, hand puppets based on animals native to the area, and plush singing birds of the region. Hours change seasonally.

A great time for art lovers to visit Stockholm is the third Saturday in July, during the *Stockholm Art Fair*. Don't miss it. This juried event, started in 1973, now includes more than one hundred local art and craft exhibitors and live music by talented local musicians. It's an art party—and it draws enormous crowds to the village park. The event's collectible posters are designed by local artists and are different each year.

Blazing fall color and the *Fresh Art Fall Tour* entice the multitudes to travel the Great River Road (Highway 35) and follow byways up the bluffs. They come to browse the artists' studios in Maiden Rock, Plum City, Durand, and Pepin, on the first weekend in October. And it happens again during the *Spring Tour*.

# Where Eagles Soar

## Upper Mississippi River Area

Along the Upper Mississippi every hour brings something new. There are crowds of odd islands, bluffs, prairies, hills, woods, and villages—everything one could desire to amuse the children. Few people ever think of going there, however.

— MARK TWAIN, *Chicago Tribune* (1886)

Where else in Wisconsin but in the backwaters of the upper Mississippi River can you watch pelicans dive, bald eagles soar, and great blue herons hold forth below? And this is just a sliver of the waterfowl that migrate through this North American corridor. Tundra swans and canvasback ducks touch down here by the thousands each spring and fall. And those many vistas from the hovering five-hundred-foot bluffs to the east of the river are both exclusive and extraordinary.

The Mississippi River valley tells its story all the way up to Lake Itasca, Minnesota, and right down to New Orleans, Louisiana. Lucky for us, many chapters run through Wisconsin's Driftless Area. But to know the river intimately you only need to take the Great River Road, Highway 35, through a few river towns like Fountain City and Alma and Pepin. Or you can take it all the way up to Prescott where the Mississippi passes the baton to the Saint Croix River just before it turns westward into Minnesota. Take the drive and get a good dose of what Mark Twain said is "everything one could desire to amuse the children." Who would argue with the Mississippi River's favorite son?

This is a road on which you won't easily find a water park that isn't naturally flowing from the river, or an amusement park that wasn't put there by a local outsider artist, or an outpost that doesn't sell primarily locally homespun goods. This trip is about the landscape and its people. This is where you can slowly move up or down the river and get a good idea of who lives on its banks and up in its bluffs and inside its valleys. And through the many books written by the locals who love this mighty river, you come away with a great sense of who their ancestors were and how this river life has sustained these cliffside hamlets for centuries.

Recreation on the river comes in many forms. Birding here is some of the best in the state. Biking along the river is on-road the entire length of this highway, but is off-road where state trails wind through parks and refuges. Ride above Highway 35 in the bluffs and you can find the loneliest of farm-side routes with heartland views so lush and expansive you might think you're in Provence. Paddling through the *Upper Mississippi National Wild-life and Fish Refuge* can be equal shares agony and ecstasy, depending upon the changes in the water level and the frequency with which the backwaters traverse the high and low wetland. But the sand islands are plentiful and the camping is free. And once you've locked through a dam or navigated the well-marked wing dams in the main river channel that keep the traffic within a safe corridor, or have watched as a barge rounds a bend marking its status as the river's most formidable vehicle, you can say you really know the people and the river they love.

## Getting There

Alma, Trempealeau, and Fountain City are across the Mississippi River, via the Winona bridge, from Winona, Minnesota, which is on the *Amtrak* Empire Builder route (Chicago to Minneapolis and on to the West Coast). If you board at a station with checked baggage hours (check online), Amtrak permits bikes to be checked as baggage in a box, for a fee.

## Where to Stay

The *Historic Trempealeau Hotel*, home of the famous Trempealeau walnut burger (see Where to Eat below), is a Highway 35 delight just twenty-two miles north of La Crosse. This riverside retreat with a mind of its own is a real intellectual. Its 1871 white clapboard, green-trimmed exterior can be seen from the river, so if you're traveling by boat, trust the "FOOD" sign just west of Lock 6 outside of La Crosse. Stop and dock. The hotel is a half-mile jaunt from the marina, but it's a short hike when you consider the river view. You can also call the hotel for a pick-up. The quaint hotel rooms are clean and cheap and authentically primitive—antique quilts and period furniture, no television, telephone, or wi-fi hookup, just like the good old days—but whitewashed charm makes up for the lack of technology. The only downside is that you'll share a bathroom. If you want a private bath, book the Pine Cottage or a Doc West House suite. Not part of the main building and not nearly as charming, both are hotel-quality comfortable. Or you can stay near the landing in one of the Trempealeau Hotel's Kingfisher motel rooms.

If you're into the music fest scene, the Reggae Fest and Blues Bash—oldies but goodies like Blue Öyster Cult—are highlights of the hotel's live music summer season. If you're not, be sure to call ahead to avoid a wall-sized speaker directed at your hotel window. Rent bikes at the hotel to cruise adjacent to Perrot State Park (see What to Do), or just hang out with the kids on the hotel's basketball court or volleyball sandlot. This hotel really takes your pace down a notch. Maybe even two.

Up the river in Fountain City, the *Hawks View Cottages and Lodges* speaks to its name with honesty. This resort, nestled bluffside, offers amazing views of the river and its surrounding woodland. The steep pitch of this property sets up this enclave of pine cottages with a fantastic river view with no sign of Fountain City below—not that it would be an unwelcome view since Fountain City is as charming as any river town could be.

Owners Laurie and Brad Nilles built their bluffside cottages with trees harvested from their Fountain City property and from Brad's boyhood farm in Rollingstone, Minnesota, just across the river. The cottages are cozy but no-frills, with hand-cut, handmade soaps from Blue Heron Soap Company in Shakopee, Minnesota, and no television to distract from this lovely wooded, river-view setting. Full kitchens make it possible to serve up meals while watching woodland animals forage for theirs right outside your window. And they do.

But the Nilleses' contribution to local sustainability doesn't stop here. After six years of growing grapes with minimal chemical pesticides just up the road from their Hawks View Cottages and Lodges, the Nilleses have launched the Seven Hawks Vineyards (see Where to Eat below). They produce several white and red varieties fermented from 100 percent Wisconsin-grown grapes and fruit, all of which come from either their own hillside

Bluffs above Alma provide an eagle's-eye view of barges locking through dams on the Mississippi River. (photo by Pat Dillon)

vineyard or communities in the area. With a tasting room and wine bar right in Fountain City, the Nilleses again contribute to its local economy and its historic significance through the renovation and use of the 1870s building that houses this new venture.

Wear good shoes. Some of the cottages have a climb of ninety or more steps, and Fountain City is a short walk down a very steep hill. But once you've landed, you'll find this is the kind of riverside town that gives midwestern hospitality its good name. And while you're there, you can check out the *Rock in the House* for only a buck. Here a fifty-five-ton boulder still stubbornly sits after tumbling five hundred feet into a local family's bedroom—that rock is now a vital part of the family's thriving economy!

Further up the river on Highway 35 is the much written about town of Alma. This town of 940 is best known as the spot where the tundra swans find respite during their spring and fall migration and where eagles hang out all year-round. And thanks to two guys with a lot of grit, there are several rental options in downtown Alma that coincide with the natural beauty of this historic river town. *Hotel de Ville* was Jeff Shilts and Dan Kordiak's original renovation project in town, which created two spaces in a 1938 Cape Cod colonial that had been through the wringer. Now it's an elegant vacation rental with a town house–style unit on one side and a spacious first-story flat on the other.

The spaces adjoin via a common door for an accommodation that can sleep up to ten. The rooms border on elegant, tastefully decorated with period furniture, granite counters, and marble bathroom fixtures. But the real deal here is that all of the spaces these guys have renovated were done with a recycle-and-reclaim mentality. With few exceptions, the structural changes were made with salvaged goods and reclaimed lumber. And where they can save and restore they do, like the restoration of the Alma Bakery that had stood dormant since 1986. Jeff and Dan have painstakingly restored it to its original splendor by updating the same equipment installed there in 1922 to meet modern health codes and standards. Currently the bakery isn't in operation. From Hotel de Ville, you can watch eagles circle and dive for dinner, or barges at Lock and Dam No. 4. Or you can just step outside and participate in the life of a river town without any hokey tourist regalia to spoil the experience.

## Where to Eat

At the *Historic Trempealeau Hotel* you can get a healthful meal and a chance to experience its locally famous vegetarian walnut burger and walnut balls firsthand (they're served in restaurants as a frozen product). The menu features local and organic produce in season, and many items border on wholesome and natural, like applesauce and cottage cheese as side order options. You can also get a hearty grilled three-Wisconsin-cheese sandwich and wash it down with a good Wisconsin-brewed beer or a bottomless cup of fair trade coffee. Eating summer lunch or dinner in this whitewashed, green-trimmed inn has a feel not unlike that of eating on Grandma's screened-in summer porch. It's loaded with charm.

In Fountain City, the *Monarch Tavern* is a good Irish pub, thanks to owner John Harrington, a fourth-generation Irish American, and his passion for his Irish heritage. But he and his wife, Lori Ahl, work hard to support their local food vendors of any heritage by shopping the farmers' markets in season and local butchers for their meat. They have also carried on the legacy of the original Fountain Brew recipe, a beer brewed in Fountain City from 1864 to 1965. Now brewed by Viking Brewery (see Chetek chapter), a family-run microbrewer in Dallas, Wisconsin, Fountain Brew is served out of the Monarch Tavern, which has run continuously under that name since the day it drew its first draft in 1864.

If it's a glass of wine you're after, the Monarch Tavern supports its neighbor *Seven Hawks Vineyards*, because this town is all about keeping the cash flow local. But you can also go to its tasting room in a historic building one block north of the Monarch.

Head up Highway 35 for big-city dining in the very small town of Alma with the magnificent river view. *Kate and Gracie's* is a historic and newly renovated space that has gone through many transformations over the years. But owners Ed Nagle and Laurie Farley, former Minneapolis restaurateurs, hit the jackpot with a place that offers a big-city, loft-style dining experience with small-town prices. And that it's directly across the street from the Mississippi River is no small detail. Nagle and Farley are committed to using locally grown and raised ingredients on their menu and cater to repeat Minneapolis road-trippers and Winona day-trippers because this kind of dining is hard to come by along the Great River Road. You'll find classic American fare and plenty of vegetarian pasta dishes.

Farther up the river about twenty miles, outside the town of Nelson, *The Stone Barn* serves artisan pizza. This may be the most healthful setting for making and eating pizza in the U.S. Owner Pam Taylor makes wood-fired brick oven pizza in her renovated, partially open-air stone barn. She uses her homemade Italian sausage and Spanish chorizo made from locally and humanely raised beef and pork and herbs she grows herself. This stone barn and these thousand acres are an unexpected site (and sight!) on which to eat possibly the greenest pizza in the state. After dinner you can peruse the antique shed of this 120-year-old farm to find quality stuff that's about the same age. Pam also supports local artists and opens up her restaurant as a gallery during the Fresh Art Fall and Spring Tours (see Local Arts).

In Pepin, the *Homemade Cafe* is a fairly new recruit but opened its doors wanting to offer diner food the old-fashioned way—truly homemade. Even the pickles and tortilla chips are made right there. The ingredients may not hail from the territory, but the homemade quality and down-home spirit of the place makes it an eatery worth checking out, even if it's just for a piece of homemade blueberry pie.

## Local Foraging

Just a short distance from the Hawks View Cottages in Fountain City is *Great River Organic Milling*, appropriately tucked into some of the greenest foothills in Wisconsin. There you can see the use of natural granite millstones in the milling process or purchase its organic products: whole grains, flour blends, specialty flours, hot cereals, and pancake and waffle mixes.

The organic dairy movement is thriving in Buffalo County, and the drive to visit a farm is as delicious as the end product. Drive (or bike) to Mondovi for a slide show of cattle grazing in lush green valleys and on family farms so remote the farmers are said to leave their land only for weddings and funerals. But some farmers in the Mondovi area are breaking the conventional mold by growing their crops with certified organic methods and raising their livestock lovingly and sustainably. *Coon Creek Family Farm* in Mondovi raises turkeys and chickens with TLC on organic land. They invite you to visit and to take home some of their sustainably grown poultry and goat's milk soap. If you sign up for their newsletter, you'll enjoy reading their observations about living the simple life surrounded by meaningful things—family, animals they love, land they respect—and the joys of being a sustainable family farm.

Further east in Osseo, *Castle Rock Organic Farms*, a family farm with a passion for farming sustainably and humanely, sells cheese, milk, and ice cream. You can visit their farmstead store daily.

## What to Do

*Perrot State Park*, a short distance from the Trempealeau Hotel, is a 1,270-acre swath of land nestled among the bluffs where the Trempealeau River meets the Mississippi River. It has twelve miles of bike paths and nine miles of cross-country ski trails; snowshoers are free to roam on any ungroomed trail. You can rent a canoe or kayak at the park and paddle a three-mile trail that winds through Trempealeau Bay.

The northern end of the park is the *Trempealeau National Wildlife Refuge*, 6,226 acres of isolated backwaters blocked from the Mississippi and Trempealeau Rivers by dikes that are controlled to mimic the natural ebb and flow of the river and provide habitat for waterfowl. These backwaters are located in the Driftless Area where the terrain is a mix of wetland, sand prairie, and bottomland forest.

### Tour Wisconsin Prairies

Less than 15 acres remain for each 10,000 acres of presettlement midwestern prairies and savannas. And of those, only 20 percent are protected. *The Prairie Enthusiasts* are a nonprofit organization dedicated to protection, preservation, management, and perpetuation of native prairies and savannas of the midwestern region. There are five Wisconsin chapters (and two proposed chapters) with a bounty of voluntourism opportunities. The Chippewa Savannas Chapter encompasses Eau Claire, Dunn, and Pepin Counties and the Coulee Region Chapter encompasses Buffalo, Jackson, La Crosse, Monroe, Trempealeau, and Vernon Counties. You can help plant and restore through field trips like one to Hill Prairie Restoration on the O'Connor Farm between Alma and Mondovi (Buffalo County) where participants work on 150 acres of prairie planted on previously cropped land.

Travel up the river about twenty miles and stand on the observation deck at Riecks Lake Park just north of downtown Alma to see for yourself what others talk about, write about, rave about. Here thousands of long-necked tundra swan beauties fuel up during their fall migration from northern Canada and Alaska to the Chesapeake Bay area. Check the Alma Tundra Swan Watch website (www.almaswanwatch.org) for information about their migration status so you can plan your arrival in Alma to coincide with theirs. The Buffalo River meets the Mississippi at Riecks Lake Park, affording twenty-eight miles of marked canoe trails. If you're ambitious, you can paddle all the way to Mondovi.

*Buena Vista Park, Overlook and Hiking Trails* in Alma is a little park with a grand view—thus the name. Hovering over the Mississippi River at five hundred feet, this park can be accessed at the south end of Second Street (look for the sign) on County Road E. Or you can hike straight up the bluff, which is a thrilling and challenging trek. Once you get to the top, the view of the river with a barge rounding the corner or eagles soaring overhead is one you won't soon forget.

Then head to *Wings over Alma* in downtown Alma, just south of Lock and Dam No. 4, where this community-backed nonprofit provides an observation deck for eagle watching and holds nature-focused art shows

**Great Wisconsin Birding and Nature Trail Map**

The *Great Wisconsin Birding and Nature Trail* is a mapped auto trail that reaches into every area of the state. Its trail for the Mississippi–Chippewa Rivers region covers thirteen of Wisconsin's western counties. A guide to the trail has full color maps and descriptions of sites, common and rare birds, and wildlife. Hard copies of the guide can be requested online, by phone (800-432-TRIP), or at Wisconsin Travel Information Centers.

The *Audubon Great River Birding Trail* is a self-guided tour that parallels both sides of the Mississippi River. The trail guide lists birding sites that are along or close to the Great River Road, such as parks, overlooks, wildlife refuges, and wildlife management areas. Maps, site descriptions, and facilities are provided along with birding tips.

featuring area artists. It sells locally made jewelry and books about the river, along with other items of local interest. The women who run this center are as thrilled to help you as they are about their beloved bald eagles.

Bike the northern end of the *Great River Road Bike Trail*. It's an on-road adventure up Highway 35 through the little towns of Nelson (see Nelson Cheese Factory), Pepin (Laura Ingalls Wilder's birthplace), Stockholm, Maiden Rock, Bay City, and Hagar City. Along the way canoers and kayakers can explore the *Tiffany Wildlife Area*, a rustic bayou-like wetland and bottomland that's home to whip-poor-will, red-shouldered hawk, cerulean warbler, wood duck, and several dozen other bird species. A huge population of wildlife lives among its 13,000 acres, which includes one of the state's largest continuous, bottomland hardwood forest. DNR conservation biologist Thomas Meyer recommends launching kayaks and canoes into any of the backwater areas of the confluence of the Chippewa and Mississippi Rivers rather than trying to penetrate the *Tiffany Bottoms State Natural Area* within the Tiffany Wildlife Area. There are boat landings on Highway 25 between Nelson and Wabasha, Minnesota, and another just north of Nelson where Highway 35 crosses the Chippewa River. A recommended trip is to start at the Highway 35 boat landing (on the east side of the river), paddle upstream toward Durand, and then drift downstream. You can also take the Chippewa Valley Motor Car to tour the Tiffany Bottoms State Natural

Area located deep inside the Tiffany Wildlife Area. The motor car is an antique open-air train that's located about four miles south of Durand on Highway 25 at Thibodeau Road. This is a favorite trip of birders or anyone who wants to get into the hard-to-access heart of this wildlife area. The motor car is owned by the *Chippewa Valley Motor Car Association* (CVMCA) but tours are organized by CVMCA sponsors, nature organizations like the Chippewa Savannas Chapter of the Prairie Enthusiasts (see sidebar) or Wings over Alma (see What to Do), and led by their naturalists. To sign up for a scheduled trip and directions to the parking lot, go to the CVMCA's website.

Canoe or kayak the Mississippi River backwaters. They're quiet and full of resting wildlife, migrating birds, and amazing panoramic views. There are two marked canoe/kayak trails in the Upper Mississippi National Wildlife Refuge–La Crosse District: Long Lake Canoe Trail, near Trempealeau, and the Goose Island Canoe Trail, near La Crosse. Brochures are available at the trailheads, the La Crosse DNR Service Center, or the La Crosse district headquarters of the Upper Mississippi Refuge.

*Local Arts*

When outsider artist Herman Rusch said that "beauty creates the will to live," he wasn't kidding, and he left the legacy to prove it. Rusch lived eleven days past his one hundredth birthday and, lucky for art lovers and wander-lusters, he left behind what kept him alive and kicking—the *Prairie Moon Sculpture Garden and Museum*, just north of Fountain City. Rusch first built a flower planter to jazz up the place, setting off a creative domino effect. From his workshop came a vast array of folk art and what was later the Prairie Moon Dance Pavilion. Ultimately he filled the grounds with sculptures made from quarry finds, scrap iron, rocks, and bricks, including a 230-foot arched fence, a life-sized rearing horse, and his own image. The museum is open only on Sunday afternoons from May to October, but you can interact with the outdoor pieces anytime. The Kohler Foundation restored the site, and the J. Michael Kohler Arts Center in Sheboygan has some Rusch pieces.

There is hardly a hamlet along this river road that doesn't claim ownership of at least a few starving artists whose work can be found scattered throughout the area. Thanks to the inventive mind of Kristine Kjos, a Milwaukee transplant who runs her Alma artisan gallery shop with the eye of the gifted textile artist that she is, much of that art can be found en masse in *The Commercial*. Kjos has a gift for merchandising her

Kristine Kjos inventively dangles lampshades as an "Open" sign at The Commercial, her art gallery in Alma. (photo by Pat Dillon)

eclectic collection, making The Commercial one of the river's most creative spots to see the work of regional artists. Kjos's partner, Tim Erickson, is a painter who creates colorful abstract landscapes while Kjos hand- and machine-stitches whimsical-to-elegant velvet and cotton textiles, constructs papier-mâché sculptures, and hand-paints and beads ornaments and other functional and decorative objects. She also does a dandy job of dangling inventive, eye-catching displays in the windows of her historic Main Street building overlooking the Mississippi River, an art show of its own. Kjos keeps her business practices local and her gallery one you simply should not miss.

*BNOX Gold and Iron* in Pepin represents a plethora of area painters, photographers, textile artists, iron workers, and jewelry makers. Owners Becky and Ted Johnson are artists and Pepin natives whose enthusiasm for their hometown and their gallery is evident from the inside out.

## Interact with Eagles

Harriet, Angel, Columbia, Donald, and Was'akas are rescued eagles that now entertain visitors at the *National Eagle Center* (www.nationaleaglecenter.org) in Wabasha, Minnesota, just across the Mississippi River from the town of Nelson. The stories of how these formidable birds came to the National Eagle Center are harrowing, and how they've acclimated impressive. Because these eagles are tethered rather than caged, visitors can interact with them while naturalists talk about the feeding habits and habitat of eagles. You may never again get this close to a bird this magnificent!

Every October and May, artist studios throughout Pepin, Pierce, and Buffalo Counties open their doors for the *Fresh Art Fall and Spring Tours*. Patrons and locals come out to see artists and their muse while driving through spectacular fall color or spring bloom, each in itself an art "installation."

# A Trail Runs through It

## Upper Saint Croix Valley Area

It is hereby declared to be the policy of the United States that certain selected rivers of the Nation which, with their immediate environments, possess outstandingly remarkable scenic, recreational, geologic, fish and wildlife, historic, cultural, or other similar values, shall be preserved in free-flowing condition, and that they and their immediate environments shall be protected for the benefit and enjoyment of present and future generations.

— Wild and Scenic Rivers Act, 1968

Long before the upper Saint Croix River became a national wild and scenic river in 1968, canoeists paddled this border river. Visitors have long been drawn to the town of Saint Croix Falls by the spectacularly beautiful geography carved by its namesake river and the dramatic views of the river gorge from Interstate State Park, Wisconsin's oldest. Away from the river, glacial lakes dotting the rolling valley edge lure travelers. Nature lovers flock to Crex Meadows Wildlife Area near Grantsburg. The upper Saint Croix valley is filled with natural beauty — and a wild and scenic river runs through it.

A series of towns that lie to the east of the river are linked by the Gandy Dancer State Trail, an old railroad bed that once carried trains north to Superior and now is traveled by bicyclists and hikers. In these small towns, thriving local art communities both enrich the area culturally with the visual arts, theater, and music and weave another thread into the intricate tapestry that is the local economy.

Sustainable agriculture is strong in the area—organic dairies, artisan cheesemakers, community-supported agriculture (CSA) farms, food co-ops, a community garden on the fairgrounds. Increasingly, area restaurants focus on local foods. In 2007, a Land Stewardship Project—the Saint Croix River Valley Buy Fresh Buy Local campaign to "reconnect food systems with ecosystems"—gave the movement added strength.

From sustainability discussion groups in Luck, Saint Croix Falls, Amery, and Osceola, to LED streetlights in Saint Croix Falls, to the sustainable remodel of a former grocery store into the growing Saint Croix library, residents of Polk County are protecting the land they cherish.

Saint Croix Falls' Autumn Fest 2010—a celebration of art, trade, and sustainable community initiatives in the Saint Croix River valley area— included a juried local art show, live music and theater, local vendors, and an exhibit titled "In a New Light: Connecting At-Risk Teens to the Saint Croix National Scenic Riverway through Nature Photography." We love it that they composted all event waste.

## Getting There

Saint Croix Falls is on the Great River Road (Highway 35), thirty-eight miles north of Hudson, which is on the *Jefferson* bus line between Milwaukee and the Twin Cities with connections to Madison and Chicago. Boxed bicycles can be checked under the coach for a fee.

## Where to Stay

*Lake Haven Lodge* is an eco-friendly vacation rental owned by Stacia and Chris Bank. The lodge, best suited to large groups, is located on five acres of land on Round Lake, a forty-acre clear water lake about twelve miles north of Saint Croix Falls. About nine miles west along a quiet country road is the little town of Luck, where you can pick up the Gandy Dancer State Trail.

The timber-framed lodge is shaded and cooled by huge oak trees, eliminating the need for air-conditioning. Stacia and Chris planed and sanded recycled boards for reuse as rustic interior paneling. Most of their five acres are left natural, and the lawn and beach are chemical free. They use earth-friendly cleaning products and detergents and recycled paper products.

Stacia and Chris explain their eco-practices to guests and invite them to help protect the environmental health of their beloved lake place. They encourage guests to use the reusable food storage containers they provide

Chris and Stacia Bank own the Lake Haven Lodge. As a high school student, Stacia started her school's first recycling program. (photo by Lynne Diebel)

rather than plastic bags, and they don't allow Styrofoam products. Stacia provides marked bins for both recyclable items and compost—and she sorts the trash to be sure. (When she was a student at Saint Croix Falls High School, she and a science teacher started the school's first recycling program.)

Lake Haven can sleep fourteen people comfortably (all bed linens and towels are included) and has two full kitchens and two bathrooms. Big enough for a large family gathering or a group retreat, the lodge's layout also makes it feel cozy for a couple as well. You'll have the place all to yourselves, as the owners don't live on the property. A popular feature for quilting and scrap-booking groups is a large lower-level workroom with custom worktables and lighting. Throughout, Stacia has decorated with appealing and personal style—old-fashioned outdoor gear and local art, including her own stunning nature photographs.

You needn't leave the lodge to get your nature fix. A deck off the upper level of the house overlooks the lake, and the rear deck, a wetland pond. Down at the sandy swimming beach, a canoe, rowboat, and paddleboat provide nonmotorized water expeditions. Bald eagles nest in one of the big oaks, loons call from the lake, and white-tail deer drink at the lake and wander the yard. Guests have spotted everything from turtles to pheasants, grouse, and fox. And at day's end, as the sun sets quietly over Round Lake, the only sound is a choral group of frogs warming up for their concert.

*Wissahickon Farms Country Inn* is on thirty acres of land on the edge of Saint Croix Falls. The rustic little cabin along the edge of a wood, far enough from the owners' house to ensure privacy, was a recycling project. Using parts of two century-old barns, a fellow named Tom Betz built the structure in the early 1980s as a replica of a frontier general store. It's made entirely of old barn boards, inside and out. Owners and innkeepers Sherilyn and Steve Litzkow acquired the cabin in 1995. Antique collectors themselves, they furnished it with dozens of authentic period pieces they already owned, including a handsome handmade quilt on the antique iron bedstead and a wringer washer on the front porch. They have a recycling program for guests, and they installed a geothermal heating and cooling system and changed all bulbs to CFLs.

Modern comforts include a queen-sized mattress on the bed, and a hide-a-bed sofa that sleeps two more. A kitchenette with a small refrigerator, microwave, coffeemaker, and buffet range makes it possible to prepare simple meals, and rental includes a continental breakfast. The bathroom of this frontier-style dwelling has a whirlpool tub. In Steve's words, this is the kind of cabin Laura Ingalls Wilder wished she lived in.

Hiking on thirty acres of land is right out the front door where the southern end of the Gandy Dancer State Trail, open to bicyclists and hikers, runs through the property. You can either head north or connect to a segment of the Ice Age Trail that runs along the Saint Croix River and links with hiking and cross-country ski trails at Interstate State Park. Sherilyn and Steve will lend snowshoes to guests.

In the little town of Alpha east of Grantsburg, the *Smoland Prairie Homestead Inn* offers three bed-and-breakfast rooms in a restored two-story hand-hewn log farmhouse built in 1869 by Swedish immigrants. A former summer kitchen recycled from another farm is now a sauna and steam room. Guests share the parlor, kitchen, dining room, dressing room, bathroom, sauna, and screened porches. Innkeepers Virginia and Joseph Hennessey raise Buelingo beef cattle and chickens on the farm, and sell fresh eggs and frozen cuts of beef (processed by Daeffler's Quality Meats in nearby Frederic) as well as Virginia's fresh-baked bread in their Kitchen Store. Best of all, Virginia teaches bread making in her farm kitchen.

You can camp along the river at *Interstate State Park* right outside Saint Croix Falls. The north campground, which has flush toilets and showers (seasonal), includes several tent sites right along the river.

## Where to Eat

If you stay at the Lake Haven Lodge, you'll have great kitchen facilities and can shop at the Natural Alternative Food Co-op in nearby Luck. See Local Foraging for more information.

Luck is fortunate to be the home of *Cafe Wren*, and visitors are equally in luck (we couldn't resist). Beyond the fair trade coffee and espresso and bakery goods made fresh daily, Stephanie Lundeen's delightful little eatery is a locavore's delight. She partners with several local growers, buying fresh all season and bushels of vegetables like squash, onions, and potatoes to store in the fall. These foods are the backbone of her menu—she estimates that in summer 60 percent of her ingredients (and over 50 percent year-round) are grown and raised within twelve miles of the cafe.

Choose the Wren's ever-changing lunch special, a bowl of delicious homemade soup served with fresh-baked ciabatta. Sandwiches and salads made with locally grown ingredients and more baked treats—like a mocha brownie to die for—round out the menu. Wash it down with a local microbrew or sip a glass of wine from nearby Trade River Winery.

There's more. As you arrive at the Wren, you'll spot the solar panels on the side of this recycled former two-story house. The solar hot water system, installed by Legacy Solar of nearby Frederic, provides at least 65 percent of its needs. Bulbs are CFLs. Stephanie recycles, composts kitchen scraps, and uses biodegradable cups and sleeves. She also displays and sells the work of local artists and features local music. The Wren is right on the Gandy Dancer Trail—how convenient is that? Most important, the food is creative and delicious.

At *Grecco's on the Saint Croix*, a restaurant in Saint Croix Falls, an expansive deck for warm weather dining overlooks the river. Inside the restored building, the ambiance is intimate and restful—a fireplace, wood floors, and local art on the walls. Owner/chef Justin Grecco lists his regional vendors on the menu: Stickney Hills Dairy, Women's Environmental Institute CSA, LoveTree Farmstead, and Keppers Produce, to name a few. He estimated that in 2010 nearly 80 percent of his produce was sourced locally during the growing season. The restaurant's beef comes from cattle raised in Minnesota and processed by Unger Meat; a bar code tells the customer which ranch their beef was raised on. The menu, which Justin calls eclectic fusion, changes weekly and includes a tasting menu every day. Justin's credentials are great—training at Le Cordon Bleu in Minneapolis and twelve years' experience in the field—and we like his commitment to serving local foods.

## Local Foraging

*Fine Acres Market* in downtown Saint Croix Falls sells local seasonal organic produce, local meats, local dairy products, local breads and cookies, bulk foods, and nutritional supplements. Eileen Jordahl shares ownership of the store with Rick and Susan Vezina, who grow much of the store's produce on their farm.

The Saint Croix Falls Farmers' Market is held in library plaza on Saturdays, June through October.

The Grantsburg Farmers' Market is held at 316 South Brad Street on Mondays, June through October.

The *Natural Alternative Food Co-op* in Luck, open since 1974, carries local organic produce, eggs, organic dairy products, bulk foods, and organic groceries.

South of Grantsburg, Doug and Kathy Anderson of *Beaver Creek Ranch* sell frozen cuts of organic beef, poultry, and hogs from the ranch. They also offer their pork as a chemical-free bacon, processed with spinach by Ye Olde Butcher Shoppe in Rochester, Minnesota, and as chemical-free hot dogs, processed with celery juice by Laurent's Meats in Cannon Falls, Minnesota. They raise interesting Scottish longhorn cattle and mulefoot pigs and still use draft horses for some of their farm work. The Andersons welcome visitors—please call first. In spring, you can visit the baby animals. In the fall, pick up gourds, pumpkins, and squash. In winter, go on a sleigh ride.

At the Burnett Dairy Cooperative in Alpha, master cheesemakers Steve Tollers and Bruce Willis craft award-winning cheeses. The *Burnett Dairy Cheese Store* in Alpha sells these tasty cheeses, as well as locally produced honey, maple syrup, wild rice, jams, eggs, and meats.

Seven miles north of Saint Croix Falls on Highway 87 is *Chateau Saint Croix Winery and Vineyard*. Troy and Laura Chamberlin are growing seven northern cold-hardy grapes—Saint Croix, Frontenac, Sabrevois, Prairie Star, E.S. 6-16-30, Marquette, and Star of the North—in a small vineyard which will eventually grow to ten acres. In 2010, only the 2008 Frontenac Port and the 2007 50/50 Frontenac/CA Cabernet Blend were made from their own grapes, but they plan to increase the list as their vines mature. Meanwhile, they truck in California and Washington grapes for their winery. Ask for the local stuff.

## What to Do

In *Interstate State Park* just south of Saint Croix Falls, you can hike nine miles of trails. The dalles of the Saint Croix River are fascinating—potholes of many sizes and a deep gorge carved by the glacial river, dramatic rock outcrops, spectacular views. The park also has two miles of snowshoe trails, eleven miles of classic groomed trails into areas accessible only during skiing season, and a shelter.

Canoe camping is the best and most exciting way to explore the wild and scenic Saint Croix River. From the mouth of the Namekagon River to Saint Croix Falls, the river is totally undeveloped (well, there is one riverside house), with primitive canoe campsites all along its length. You can find out more at the *Saint Croix National Scenic Riverway Visitor Center* headquarters in Saint Croix Falls. At *Wild River Outfitters*, an excellent company in Grantsburg. Jerry Dorff and Marilyn Chesnik offer canoe and kayak rentals, maps and trip planning, and shuttle service. Mike Svob's *Paddling Northern Wisconsin* includes detailed route descriptions and maps.

The *Gandy Dancer State Trail* runs from Saint Croix Falls north for forty-seven miles to Danbury through the towns of Centuria, Milltown, Luck, Frederic, Lewis, Siren, and Webster. From April through November, use is limited to biking and hiking, and a bike pass is required. In each town, restrooms are located near the trail. What's a gandy dancer, you ask? Back in the day, railroad crews used hand tools made by the Gandy Tool Company. As they worked, they synchronized the rhythmic swinging of these tools with musical chants—thus the nickname and its application to this trail, a former railroad bed.

On the east edge of Luck, the Chippewa Trail is a great little biking route during spring wildflower season and fall color. From the state trail, ride east on Butternut Avenue. Turn right on Seventh Street at the school, then angle left onto South Shore Drive, then turn right on South Lake (150th) Street. Turn left on Golf Course Road/Chippewa Trail and follow it, heading straight onto the marked road (Rustic Road No. 93), which runs for three miles to its end at County Road GG.

*Straight Lake State Park* is 3.5 miles off Highway 35 at the end of 270th Avenue, northeast of Luck. Dedicated in 2005, the park is still being managed

### Explore Wild Wisconsin with the Experts

Wisconsin has more than its share of natural beauty. Sample the wealth on field trips that connect you to what Jeffrey Potter of the *Natural Resources Foundation of Wisconsin* (NRF) calls the heart and soul of Wisconsin. For more than twenty years, the foundation has worked with citizens, businesses, nonprofit organizations, and the government to promote the protection and enjoyment of Wisconsin's public lands, waters, and wildlife. NRF field trips offer expert guides, one-of-a-kind experiences, and remarkably low prices, making these trips among the best outdoor activities in the state. We love these outdoor adventures.

Trips are led by Wisconsin Department of Natural Resources conservation biologists and others who share their love and knowledge of the state's natural resources with participants. Nearly one hundred trips are offered statewide between April and October each year. Registration for all trips opens in the spring and continues throughout the season, but space is limited and some trips fill quickly. Members can register for members-only trips and have priority during registration. You can become a member, learn more about the program, and register for field trips on the foundation's website.

---

by Interstate State Park. For now, there's an unmarked parking area and only foot traffic is allowed. The Ice Age Trail (www.iceagetrail.org) now runs into and through the park, and you can explore several miles of trails around the lake and the flowages. The crystal clear flowages are great for swimming. Or carry in a canoe or boat—it's a good place to teach kids to paddle or fish. This park's a lovely spot, a quiet little treasure.

North of Grantsburg, *Crex Meadows Wildlife Area* is a vast nature preserve: thirty thousand acres of wetlands, brush prairie, native prairie, and flowages. This marshy land, a gift from the last glacier, is home to more than 270 species of birds, half of which nest there. There are breeding populations of ospreys, eagles, trumpeter swans, Karner blue butterflies, Blanding's turtles, and red-necked grebes. A breeding pack of timber wolves lives here. During fall migration, flocks of thousands of sandhill cranes rest here. It's an amazing example of successful eco-restoration. After the land was purchased by the state in 1946, it was gradually transformed from a logged-over, drained-out, ecological mess to its current natural beauty. To get there, follow the series of flying geese painted on the streets of Grantsburg to the visitor center where you can learn more about the area. Pick up a free self-guided auto tour booklet describing a twenty-four-mile loop route—for bicyclists as well—with historical information and lists of wildlife. If you're comfortable in a kayak and slogging through bogs on foot, consider helping with a Trumpeter Swan Cygnet Roundup and Banding, a Natural Resources Foundation of Wisconsin (see the sidebar) field trip held each August (sign up in March as soon as registration opens, as the trip fills fast). If this one sounds too strenuous, NRF holds other field trips at Crex Meadows—participants in 2011 monitored bats, observed dragonflies, and collected frogs.

Northwest of Grantsburg is the *Brandt Pines Ski Trail*, located in Governor Knowles State Forest. Ten miles of cross-country ski trails—groomed for classic only—loop through old growth pine forest along the Saint Croix River. The trails are also open to hikers, and there's an interpretive trail.

## Local Arts

The *Saint Croix Festival Theatre* is in a beautifully restored vaudeville playhouse on the main street of Saint Croix Falls. Built in 1917, the building had fallen on hard times by the late 1980s. Starting in 1989, scores of volunteers working endless hours cleaned and redecorated. The Saint Croix Festival Theatre was launched in 1990 and has produced over one hundred plays since it opened. Renovation efforts continued—think velvet and leather seats with lots of leg room—and in 2007 the building was named to the National Register of Historic Places.

Restored to its original glory, the playhouse is now a treasure, offering professional theater in an intimate setting. The calendar includes theater and music series and some great special events. The Youth and Family Theatre Series offers classes and workshops taught by the director, two professional actors, the stage manager, and a designer. Other classes and workshops focus on musical theater for teens and summer creativity camps.

After occupying a corner of the theater building for many years, in 2009 the *Saint Croix Falls Public Library* moved to a recycled grocery store building that had stood empty for eleven years. Using local and recycled materials

## Intentional Community

Osceola is south of Saint Croix Falls, and south of Osceola is the *Community Homestead*, dedicated to living and working with people with special needs. It has recently built a beautiful new community center with materials from the farm and recycled materials—stones from the river valley for the fireplace, floor boards from an old mill in Saint Croix Falls, and ceiling boards and beams from a nearby barn.

Visitors are welcome to tour the large organic CSA farm, orchard, and dairy; furniture and crafts workshops; and organic bakery. During the summer, groups may arrange longer service-learning projects like the three-day Waldorf group camp. Events at the community center are open to the public—a spring craft fair and a summer folk dance and pig roast.

In addition to on-farm sales, the Community Homestead sells baked goods and produce at the Osceola Farmers' Market and Fine Acres Market in Saint Croix Falls and crafts in gift shops in Saint Croix Falls. Contact the community for information on custom furniture crafted from locally grown hardwoods.

A CSA hoop house at Community Homestead is filled with new growth in the spring. (photo by Lynne Diebel)

and local labor, the town installed a passive thermal solar array to fuel radiant floor heat, high efficiency water fixtures, and a lighting control system that reduces lighting expense by 80 percent during daylight hours. With volunteer labor, the library collection was moved in less than a week. The new library expands the Becky Prichard Collection, emphasizing conservation and environmentalism, and showcases native son Gaylord Nelson's papers. The library teamed up with the *Saint Croix Scenic Coalition* and *Saint Croix Scenic Byway*, environmental education and advocacy groups that share an office in the new building, to provide print and digital resources to library patrons.

*Earth Arts of the Upper Saint Croix Valley*, a group of local artists and artisans based in Saint Croix Falls, hosts a big studio tour the first weekend in May. The Spring Art Tour of the upper Saint Croix valley is a wonderful chance for you to chat with artists in their studios, watch demonstrations, and buy cool local art. On Saturday of the same weekend, the *West Denmark Lutheran Church* near Luck holds its annual Aebleskiver Dinner, open to the public. Why not do both? (Just in case you're curious, *Aebleskiver* is Danish for apple pancake.) The Earth Arts Fall Art Salon—an exhibition of work created around a theme and displayed at the Cafe Wren Community Room in Luck—features a reception for all the artists.

On the main street of Saint Croix Falls at the *Luhrs/Björnson Artworks*, the pottery and blown glass of Leif Björnson and the watercolors and pastels of Margaret Luhrs are on display (like her lovely watercolor of a red canoe beside the Saint Croix). Leif's working studio is in the gallery. Housed in a historic granary building restored by the artists, the gallery overlooks one of the oldest hydroelectric dams in the country. We like only dams that earn their keep.

North of Saint Croix Falls at *Blackberry Hills*, Loretta and Jerry Pederson raise fiber animals—sheep, alpacas, and llamas—and teach one-day spinning classes and weekend weaving and dyeing workshops. If you're interested in visiting their beautiful farm and inspiring studio, check the website for open studio dates or call ahead to set a different date. Meet the animals; see handcrafted shawls, scarves, ponchos, and hats; and find new yarns for your own fiber projects. Loretta sells handmade goat's milk soap—a luxurious little gift.

Blackberry Hills products are also available at Chateau Saint Croix Winery and Vineyard and at *Mrs. I's Yarn Parlor* in Osceola, which features locally grown, spun, and dyed yarns from a number of farms—definitely worth a visit.

Artist Leif Björnson works in his Saint Croix Falls studio, a recycled granary with a view of the Saint Croix River. (photo by Lynne Diebel)

In August, the Saint Croix Band of Lake Superior Chippewa (Ojibwe) holds the annual *Saint Croix Wild Rice Pow-wow*. The three-day celebration, with Native American dancing, drumming and singing, and traditional Native American food and art, is held at Saint Croix Casino in Danbury, also known as Hole-in-the-Wall Casino.

# Northeast Wisconsin

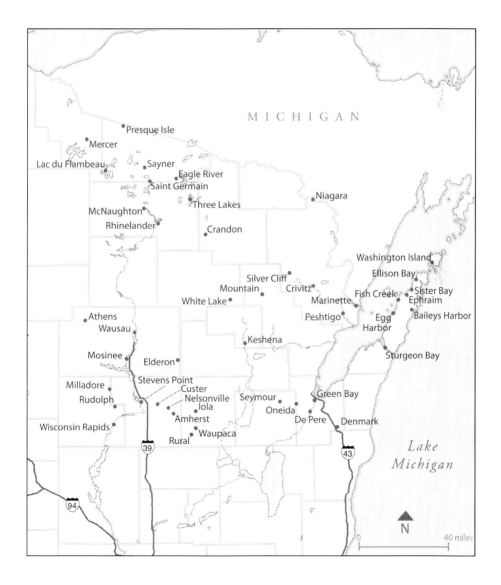

MICHIGAN

Presque Isle
Mercer
Lac du Flambeau
Sayner
Eagle River
Saint Germain
Niagara
Three Lakes
McNaughton
Rhinelander
Crandon

Washington Island

Silver Cliff
Ellison Bay
Mountain
Crivitz
Sister Bay
White Lake
Marinette
Ephraim
Fish Creek
Athens
Peshtigo
Baileys Harbor
Wausau
Egg Harbor
Mosinee
Keshena
Elderon
Sturgeon Bay
Stevens Point
Milladore
Custer
Rudolph
Nelsonville
Iola
Seymour
Green Bay
Amherst
Oneida
Wisconsin Rapids
Waupaca
De Pere
Denmark
Rural

Lake
Michigan

N

40 miles

# Renewable Energy Pioneers

## *Amherst Area*

It's a good way to live.

—MARGUERITE RAMLOW, Artha Sustainable Living Center

Who wouldn't want to visit the land where the Tomorrow River flows? Eastern Portage County can also make you remember yesterday—the time when rural roads were narrow, shoulderless byways winding through quiet country-side. Once off the main highway, you still get that feeling. You'll find it east of the busy university town of Stevens Point, where the terrain undulates softly, a gift from the glaciers that scoured the land ten thousand years ago. This is kettle country, where clear lakes fill bowl-shaped depressions left by the melting of buried glacial ice. Low sandy rises—often wooded—are interspersed with small fields and meadows. Fencerows of boulders, the rocky glacial litter cleared by settlers, follow the curving roads. It's a land-scape of gentle green beauty.

And it's an area devoted to sustainable living. In 2008, the city of Stevens Point joined Wisconsin's growing list of eco-municipalities. From Stevens Point east to Waupaca, there's a deeply rooted community of folks who embraced and lived green long before it became a buzz word. Many got their inspiration from the nationally renowned conservation and environmental education programs of the University of Wisconsin–Stevens Point. The Midwest Renewable Energy Association (MREA) has headquarters in nearby

Custer. Drawn by the annual MREA Energy Fair, over twenty-three thousand people descended on little Custer in 2010.

There's more. Jim McKnight and Mark Klein, owners of Amherst-based Gimme Shelter Construction, have designed and built high-performance homes—including their own—for more than twenty-five years. Mark's a founding member of MREA. James Kerbel, owner of Photovoltaic Systems southwest of Amherst and also a founding member of MREA, has been installing photovoltaic energy systems for even longer. Central Waters Brewing Company in Amherst, owned and operated by Paul Graham and Anello Mollica, is the state's first green-powered brewery. The Stevens Point–based Central Rivers Farmshed helps create a local food economy by building and strengthening relationships among farmers, restaurant owners, retailers, and consumers in central Wisconsin and hosts events on environmental topics at the Tomorrow River Chautauqua in Amherst.

Bob and Marguerite Ramlow, owners of Artha Sustainable Living Center south of Amherst and founding members of MREA, have been in the solar energy business since the 1970s. Bob is a solar thermal technical lead for Wisconsin's Focus on Energy, helping residents and businesses install cost-effective projects for energy efficiency and renewable energy. He wrote a book on solar water and space heating systems—coauthored by his son-in-law, Benjamin Nusz—and teaches nationwide. He also offers hands-on solar installation workshops at the Artha Center. Their daughter, Chamomile Nusz, works in the business as well.

Offering energy and renewal in other forms, Marguerite teaches yoga, herbal medicine, organic gardening, and food preservation workshops. And together with their son, Leif Ramlow, and Chamomile, they run a very green bed-and-breakfast.

## Getting There

Amherst is ten miles from Waupaca, which is on the *Lamers* bus line's daily route between Milwaukee and Wausau.

## Where to Stay

Seven miles south of Amherst, the *Artha Sustainable Living Center*, with the second highest Travel Green Wisconsin certification, is powered by the sun. Solar installations that power and heat the Ramlows' separate straw bale house—featured in *Mother Earth News*—also power the yoga studio and the farmhouse where bed-and-breakfast guests stay. Solar energy is harnessed in the one-third acre organic garden that feeds the Ramlows and their guests all year. And solar energy flows from the 150 maple trees that the family and friends tap for syrup on their ninety-acre farmstead.

The renovated two-story farmhouse—rentable daily or weekly year-round—has three guest rooms, one of which is upstairs. Solar energy helps to heat the house's hot water and provide electricity. Furnishings are simple, comfortable, and lovely. The Ramlows painted the whole interior with non-VOC paint and provide organic cotton towels and sheets. Guests share the first-floor bathroom—low-flow toilet, old-fashioned claw-foot tub, and low-flow showerhead—and light-filled kitchen, living room, and sun room. There's a spacious deck for all to share as well. Workshop space is in the yoga studio, a straw bale barn. In warm weather, yoga workshops are held in a gazebo.

*Amherst Riverdance*, on the outskirts of Amherst and on the banks of the Tomorrow/Waupaca River, is a vacation rental certified by Travel Green Wisconsin. Owners Chuck and Mary Egle handcrafted the cabin. On the outside, it looks like a typical Northwoods log cabin, until you spot the iron spiral staircase they rescued from a foundry and repurposed as a second-floor fire escape and tiny balcony. Inside, the same whimsy plays out in imaginative details: an entire tree trunk is the center of the two-story spiral staircase and an upside-down stump, roots and all, is the base for a bathroom sink. The house sleeps eight in three bedrooms and a loft, and there are two bathrooms, one with a whirlpool tub. There's a fully equipped kitchen and a big dining table. The setting isn't isolated. Several neighbors' homes and State Highway 10 are clearly visible from the property. But the Egles have restored the surrounding ten acres to native prairie and oak savanna, and a short path leads from the back deck down to a lovely wooded stretch of the Tomorrow/Waupaca, where guests can kayak, canoe, or cast for trout. There's a canoe for guests to use.

The Egles built green because that's the way they think. They're especially fond of recycling. "We find these things that we like, and then we figure out how to reuse them," Mary said about the foundry staircase. Incorporated into the house are: radiators from a mansion in Stevens Point; massive beams from the Lullaby Furniture Company in Stevens Point; French doors from a remodeling job in Plover; counters, tabletop, and bench hand-hewn from an oak that fell in a storm; and timbers and planks from a dismantled barn in Menominee. The Egles insulated the roof with open cell foam made from castor oil, and the walls and foundation with closed cell foam. Solar panels heat the water for the taps, the radiators, and the radiant heat pipes below the brick and tile floors.

Across the road stands the Cameron House, nominated to the National Register of Historic Places as one of the area's oldest buildings. In 2002, when it stood in the way of the expansion of U.S. Highway 10, Chuck and Mary rescued the worn out house from destruction by moving it to its current location and rebuilding it. One thing led to another, and they rescued a barn as well. Both are now used by UW–Stevens Point for Learning Is ForEver (LIFE) classes on topics like invasive plants, native woods, and gardening. The Egles, who also own a landscaping business, built a labyrinth on the land. And then they built the Riverdance Cabin. As Mary said, Chuck never met a project he didn't like.

## Where to Eat

If you're an Artha guest, you're invited to graze freely in the organic garden and cook in the B&B's artful, well-equipped kitchen. Riverdance has a great kitchen as well. You'll also find an eatery that serves local foods, a local bakery, and a very green brewpub in the village of Amherst.

At *Morning Star Coffee and Bistro*, longtime Amherst resident and owner Kelly Koch supports eating local. He estimates that in summer about half of his ingredients are locally sourced. The bistro serves breakfast and lunch: coffee and smoothies, homemade bakery goods, soups and sandwiches, daily specials, meals to go, Central Waters beer, and imported wines. Every Sunday morning, there's a breakfast buffet. Once a month, Kelly offers a five-course Lamp Lit Dinner that draws both locals and folks from Milwaukee and Appleton. Call the bistro for dates and reservations. In 2010, Kelly and the local fire department organized Celebrate Amherst, a village-wide festival held in September to showcase local food producers, artists, and artisans.

On North Main Street in Amherst, *New Village Bakery* owner David Ryles bakes homemade breads and pastries with recipes reflecting his Scottish heritage.

If you like a great microbrew, Amherst is the place to go. (Beer's a food, right?) Enjoy a pint at the tap room of *Central Waters Brewing Company*, recently remodeled with all recycled materials, including boards and corrugated metal from a nearby aged barn. Located in the Amherst Business Park, it's open Fridays and Saturdays, and often draws a crowd of over a hundred, with the regulars arriving a tad early to set up the bar stools. Look

Anello Mollica, co-owner of Central Waters Brewing Company, holds a pint of Shine On, a red ale created to celebrate the brewery's commitment to solar power and its association with the Midwest Renewable Energy Association. (photo by Robert Diebel)

### Granola, from Artha Bed and Breakfast

4 cups old-fashioned oats
1 cup coarsely chopped nuts (cashews, pecans, or almonds)
1 cup raw (unroasted) sunflower seeds
1/2 cup sesame seeds
1/2 cup shredded unsweetened coconut
1/2 teaspoon sea salt
6 tablespoons maple syrup
6 tablespoons canola oil
1 cup raisins, dried bananas, or any other dried fruit you like

Preheat oven to 300 degrees. Toss the oats, nuts, sunflower seeds, sesame seeds, coconut, and salt to mix in a large bowl. Pour maple syrup and oil over the oat mixture. Stir with a spoon until all is moistened. Spread-about 1/2-inch thick on baking sheets and roast for 30 to 40 minutes, stirring occasionally, until golden. Cool thoroughly, then stir in dried fruits. Store in a glass jar. We serve this in a wine glass as a parfait, layered with yogurt, strawberries, raspberries, and bananas. Our guests at the B&B love it. I hope you enjoy it too.
Peace,

—Marguerite Ramlow

for the solar array, visible from the Highway 10 overpass. Great beer's the draw, of course. Paul Graham and Anello Mollica's Bourbon Cherry Stout won a gold medal at the 2006 Great American Beer Festival. But so is the sustainability ethic. These earth-friendly brewers installed twenty-four solar panels for hot water and radiant floor heat, and their brewing equipment has an energy-saving heat exchanger, drastically reducing the amount of natural gas they now use and gaining them recognition as Wisconsin's first green-powered brewery. An on-site grain silo reduces packaging waste. They recycle all their spent grains to local organic farmers for livestock feed and compost. Together with four other microbreweries, they launched a state-wide hops and barley cooperative to support Wisconsin grain production rather than buying from out of state. A portion of the sales of Shine

On—Irish red ale brewed with barley grown five miles down the road—is donated to the MREA, and the brew's name pays homage to their shared solar energy commitment. They're considering a wind turbine for the future. Tours are by appointment, so call ahead.

## Local Foraging

Nearby Waupaca has a farmers' market (see Local Foraging in the Waupaca chapter.)

## What to Do

Artha Center workshops and retreats are offered year-round—a current calendar is posted on their website. Groups may rent the studio (as well as the entire B&B) for their own workshops, retreats, and family gatherings.

Yoga instruction includes a wide range of half-day and full-day yoga workshops and weekend yoga retreats for all levels. Artha also holds a spring Door County Yoga Retreat weekend.

Organic gardening classes are interactive—you'll get dirt on your hands while learning about "Planning and Planting Your Vegetable Garden." Marguerite also teaches the hands-on "Harvesting and Storing Food from the Garden." Herbal workshops include such classes as "Herbal Medicine and Teas," "Herbal Facial Products," and "Spring Tonics"—you'll create and take home your own herbal products and recipes.

Solar workshops are also hands-on—the MREA "Solar Water Heating Installation Lab" is a three-day workshop; "Living Sustainably," a half-day. Artha's website has all the details.

One of the big lures of this area is its natural beauty, and another is the *Midwest Renewable Energy Fair*, held in Custer in June every year since 1990. Yes, folks around here have been working on alternative energy methods for a long time; the rest of us are just catching up. In 2010, the fair featured speakers, over 200 workshops, and over 275 exhibits. There was live music, food (all served on reusable or biodegradable plates, which, with the food waste, were composted), and great beer on tap from Amherst's Central Waters Brewery. Brews were served in real beer glasses—which you could take home or return for your deposit. Many folks arrived at the fair by car pool, mass transit from various cities, or shuttles from Stevens Point.

Whether or not you attend the fair, touring the *Midwest Renewable Energy Association* headquarters in Custer is a great way to learn about the latest in renewable energy technology. Its ReNew the Earth Institute is a demonstration site and educational facility. You can see working renewable energy systems and educational displays: wind electric systems with monitoring equipment and a 20kW turbine, stand-alone and tracking photovoltaic systems, a masonry stove, prairie plantings, a solar-powered pond, an off-grid photovoltaic-powered refrigerator, solar water heating, a solar hydronic floor-heating system, and straw bale and rammed tire demonstration walls. Its landscaping won the Audubon Society's Backyard Habitat award for water conservation and plant diversity. It uses renewable energy for 80 percent of its needs, has restored monoculture pine plantations, and uses organic and fair trade products. You can take a self-guided tour of the facilities and renewable energy systems.

For in-depth learning, choose from an extensive list of workshops on a variety of topics in renewable energy, ranging from half-day introductory courses to intensive seven-day hands-on installation workshops. Workshops are held in Custer, in other Wisconsin locations, and around the Midwest.

For a bit of decadence, attend Amherst's fall *Festival of Chocolate*. In addition to overindulging in chocolate delectables, you can attend such programs as "Living in Harmony" and "Growing Up Green"; take a class in belly dancing, pilates, or yoga; and enjoy local music and art.

Biking the back roads is a popular way to explore this lovely countryside. Among the interesting destinations is *Pickerel Lake State Natural Area*, south of the Artha Center on County A. It has oak uplands that were once oak savanna and a lakeshore that provides habitat for specialized plants like boneset, Kalm's lobelia, heart's-ease, silverweed, common false foxglove, and eastern willow-herb. Three miles north of Nelsonville, the *Richard A. Hemp State Fishery Area* is one of the best warbler habitats in Wisconsin. Out of thirty species seen, eighteen are documented as breeding. The maple forests and river areas of this 1,375-acre site produce an exceptional spring wildflower display and are home to Karner blue butterflies and golden eagles.

On Monday and Wednesday evenings from May through September, the *Heartland Bike and Nordic Ski Club* meets at the *Iola Scandinavia Fitness and Aquatic Center* for moderate paced, recreational rides of twenty to thirty miles, led by locals who know the area. Ambitious bicyclists can ride to Iola. Follow the Tomorrow River State Trail (see below) from Amherst to Scandinavia, and then head north on County Road G to Iola.

## Is It Tomorrow?

The Tomorrow River can confuse visitors. Upstream of Amherst, it's the Tomorrow. Downstream of Amherst, after Bear Creek flows in, bridge signs say it's the Tomorrow/Waupaca. After it flows into Waupaca County, it's just the Waupaca. But it's all the same river, under different names. The DNR's official name for the river is the Tomorrow/Waupaca; that is, until it crosses the county line. Whatever names you call it, it's a popular Class 1 trout stream from the fishery upstream of Nelsonville down to the Amherst millpond, and a Class 2 trout stream downstream of Amherst. Guests at Riverdance (see Where to Stay) need only walk out the back door to cast a line. For information on paddling the stream, see What to Do.

---

The *Tomorrow River State Trail* runs from Cate Park, on the north side of Amherst, west to Plover, with a one-mile gap at Amherst Junction where riders use local roads; and east through Scandinavia to Manawa. There's a parking area at the corner of Pond Street (County Road A) and Yellow Brick Road. The 29-mile rail trail is crushed limestone with a level grade. A trail pass is required for riders sixteen years old or older.

For canoeists and kayakers, there's a nice four-mile paddling route on the Tomorrow River, from Nelsonville to Amherst. In Nelsonville, the stream is only ten feet wide by the Rising Star Mill, a summer theater. By the time you take out at the boat landing above the dam in Amherst, the Tomorrow has widened into Amherst Pond. And there's another old mill to admire. We recommend a bike shuttle. For more information on this route, and routes downstream of Amherst, read Mike Svob's *Paddling Southern Wisconsin*. If you stay at Amherst Riverdance, the river is right out your back door. Just upstream, under the Keener Road bridge, the Eclipse Mill stood until the 1950s. Here, the river drops three feet, not for the beginning paddler.

Every fall, the Jensen Community Center in Amherst sponsors *Lettie's River Run*, with a 5K run and 5K walk along some of the area's lovely rural roads. You'll cross the Tomorrow River twice, and Central Waters Brewery will be serving beverages at the finish.

At *Standing Rocks Park*, about nine miles northwest of the Artha Center, cross-country skiers will find ten miles of trails groomed for diagonal stride-and-skate skiing as well as great views and a lodge. In summer, Standing Rocks Park has a disc golf course and mountain biking trails, with the same hills to climb and the same beautiful views.

## Local Arts

Many artists and artisans, drawn by the area's natural beauty, have settled around Amherst. Elizabeth Zenk and James Trebatoski's *Tomorrow River Gallery* on Main Street in Amherst showcases the best of these. The art includes mixed fiber works by Francie Ginocchio, pastels by Fred Ginocchio, raku pottery by Rick Foris, and painting and photography by John Davenport, among many others. During the fall *Hidden Studios Art Tour*, you can visit the studios of these and other artists in an area centered on Amherst. Liz and James also raise and sell organic plants and fresh cut flowers in season as well as garden décor—locally handmade, often from

Elizabeth Zenk, co-owner of the Tomorrow River Gallery, displays and sells the work of local artists and artisans. (photo by Robert Diebel)

recycled materials. Studio C upstairs is a multipurpose classroom and gallery space.

Liz told us the interesting history of the gallery's renovated building, which was originally a bank. Built in the late nineteenth century on the site of Amherst's current bank, the building was moved to its current location in 1907. The one-block move took five days, during which time the bank opened for business every day. For the next sixty years, it was the home of the bank, the village post office, and then the local newspaper, the *Amherst Advocate*. In the 1960s, a poet bought the building, newspaper presses and all, and it became a poetry press and the site of poetry readings, including one by Gary Snyder. Recycling has been around for a long time.

Across Main Street, Jacque Templin and Maud LaMarche own the *Wisconsin Wool Exchange*, a mecca for fiber crafters. Skeins of locally raised fibers—angora, alpaca, Shetland, merino, Icelandic—fill the storefront: Kimmet Croft Fibers of Wisconsin Rapids, Heartbreak Farms of Amherst, Wildflower Farm of Rosholt, Peaceful Pastures Alpacas. You don't have to be a knitter to love this place. Kimmet Croft's thick wool socks—made with local fiber on an antique hand-powered knitting machine—sell for less than twenty dollars a pair. And if the beauty and textures of the yarns inspire you to learn a fiber craft, the Wool Exchange offers all the tools for knitting, crocheting, spinning, and felting, as well as books and classes to get you started.

The *Rising Star Mill* in Nelsonville has a summer schedule of concerts and other cultural events, listed online.

# Arts and Orchards
# of the Door Peninsula

## *Door County*

In returning, if only now and then, to the wilderness or some semblance of it, we become citizens of the earth. It is not only our environment that we learn about, but ourselves.

—MARTY and NANCY DRURY, Ecology Sports, Sister Bay

Door County lies between Lake Michigan to the east and the lake's Green Bay to the west. It's a mix of pastoral landscapes, cherry and apple orchards, vineyards, and marine life to rival New England's shores if you can get past the lack of salt in the air. The county is named after the strait between the Door Peninsula and Washington Island, a passage littered with shipwrecks. The hazards, well known to early French explorers and local Native Americans, prompted the French appellation *Porte des Morts*, or "Death's Door."

Because of its location between Green Bay and Lake Michigan, its warm days and cool nights make it a climate perfect for growing fruit. Today locals are proud advocates of their fruit crops, a supportive foundation for a healthy economy. You can't set foot on the peninsula without considering a Ball jar of something cherry found below a rim of canning wax—jam, jelly, chutney, salsa, even pasta sauce. And who can resist following at least once a sign that directs traffic to a nearby orchard or farmers' market for a bag of produce. Vineyards abound, both fruit and grape varieties, and how nicely a Baileys Harbor–produced Chardonnay pairs with a Peninsula State Park–rendered plein air painting of a sunset over Green Bay—enough are painted annually to hang over every living room fireplace in the state. Art and artists are abundant here.

The Door County Visitor Bureau boasts of forty-one galleries from Sturgeon Bay to Washington Island, and that doesn't include the hundreds of independent artist studios tucked in and around narrow lakeside roads, many of which are housed in buildings and barns original to the peninsula. Clay is big here, too, with pottery studios and shops on both sides of the peninsula yielding every conceivable type of functional and decorative claywork. But it's Door County's most famous feature, Lake Michigan, that cannot be ignored, with its ultramarine horizon line and its 250 miles of shoreline. It laps along five state parks and most of thirteen county parks and rolls out endlessly along twenty-eight sandy beaches.

This scenario creates ripe opportunity for four-season sports activities—biking, hiking, kayaking, sailing, snowshoeing, cross-country skiing, and birding—all endeavors that use wind and human power as their predominant energy source. And while green cuisine is a little scarce on the peninsula, there is movement in that direction, especially in Jacksonport and Egg Harbor. Dining on locally raised meat is a little tricky, but at least one organic produce grower makes his good food accessible to travelers and locals alongside other healthful items at an Egg Harbor grocery store owned by his partner. You just need to know where to go.

## Where to Stay

Set central to the small artsy villages that are tucked up one side of the Door Peninsula and down the other is the whitewashed and airy, wind-powered *Lodgings at Pioneer Lane* in Ephraim. A Travel Green Wisconsin–certified business, it produces very clean energy and its buildings are naturally cool because they are close to the lake. This sweet little enclave of New England–style buildings benefits from fresh lake winds that waft through their sashed windows, making it easy to say no to cranking up the air conditioner (which is provided) even in July. After dark, a Mayberry Carriage Clydesdale clomps past, taking guests from one end of the village to the other. To say the sound of hooves on concrete "harkens back" to an earlier time would not be a cliché . . . it truly does.

Helen's Room Suite at the Lodgings at Pioneer Lane is housed in what is said to be the oldest building on the peninsula. (© 2009 Kathleen Thorne-Thomsen)

The original plank walls are exposed in the sitting room in Helen's Room Suite at the Lodgings at Pioneer Lane. (© 2009 Kathleen Thorne-Thomsen)

And if sustainability can be measured by simple offerings that produce little waste but much serenity in a lovely setting, owners Hugh and Alicia Mulliken have accomplished it. Alicia buys locally and with a conscience. In Ellison Bay's Clay Bay soap containers, she provides liquid soap made by displaced women in Illinois learning a trade. It is also in larger containers on the shower wall. The room's rag rugs are by Wisconsin weavers, sold out of Gills Rock's Farm Studio Gallery.

Little goes into the wastebasket since most of what's stocked in the room is reusable. Mulliken chooses china plates and coffee cups, real wine glasses, and flatware over plastic or disposables, with nothing to unwrap and pitch except two optional plastic cups in the bathroom. And, thank heavens, toilet tissue made of recycled paper. While you won't find a recycling bin in your room, the Mullikens separate the trash from recyclables after guests leave.

The rooms maintain the historic integrity of the 1850s, when the buildings were erected. For instance, Helen's Room, housed in what is thought to be the oldest building in Ephraim, still has the exposed split-log walls. The main building houses guest rooms upstairs and retail spaces downstairs, and stands now as one can imagine it did when the Moravians settled in Ephraim. Their migration is well documented architecturally through a self-guided walking tour of the town.

The lodge's location puts you central to the kind of nonmotorized activity the area is known for. You can rent bikes from the lodge and take them up to Washington Island or walk across the street to rent a kayak at the Door County Ephraim Kayak Center. Take the Highway 42 bike lanes in either direction to shop or view art galleries. The Lodgings at Pioneer Lane may be one of the best locations on the peninsula for travelers concerned about their carbon footprint, and the rates for these beautifully appointed rooms and suites are a bargain by many standards.

Across the peninsula is the *Whitefish Bay Farm* bed-and-breakfast, located near Whitefish Dunes State Park on the north end of Sturgeon Bay right off Highway 57. This setting is truly pastoral and serene. Its website shows a rainbow crossing the back forty, and when you're standing there on a clear day, a rainbow is not hard to imagine. The farm, a 1908 American Foursquare farmhouse, has four guest rooms and is resort-style clean. The surrounding landscape is groomed but rugged with a knotty patchwork of pastures and trails on which a herd of Corriedale sheep get rotated regularly.

Gretchen and Dick Regnery raise their white and natural Corriedale sheep sustainably, and with a loving hand. If you arrive on a day when the lambs and their mothers have been separated, you will find the Regnerys allowing the mothers time and space to adjust by keeping guests at a quiet or respectful distance. It might break your heart, but they will tell you that an alternative approach would be more stressful. The sheep yield yarn that Gretchen spins into skeins to sells on their website or felts into small functional works. Dick weaves the wool into amazing blankets, and both Gretchen and Dick sell their work out of their art gallery in a converted barn where they also represent a number of other Door County artists. Breakfast at the farm is a mix of grown-on-the-farm fruit and vegetables and eggs. What the Regnerys don't pick fresh themselves, they get from other local growers. This B&B is far from the Door County crowds but close enough to find them if you need a people fix or if you come for the art and culture along with the nature and serenity. The Whitefish Bay Farm B&B is also where the Door County Shepherds Market is held each year. This is northeastern Wisconsin's oldest fiber event and sale. Whitefish Dunes State Park, an 865-acre park along Lake Michigan, is located across County Road WD from the farm (see What to Do for more information).

## Where to Eat

If you haven't been to *The Cookery* restaurant since its devastating fire in 2008, you might not recognize its new face. Owned by Dick and Carol Skare, the Cookery is a Fish Creek casual dining institution that the Skares defined as "green" even before their renovation took the business from a clapboard diner to a state-of-the-art, two-story stone building with reclaimed hardwood floors. Members of the Travel Green Wisconsin certification program before the fire, the Skares trace their philosophy to the sustainable farm on which Carol grew up, where nothing was wasted and the land was respected. When they were forced to close their doors, local businesses came forward and put the salvaged canned Door County cherry products the Cookery is known for on their own shelves. Once again you can enjoy loads of Wisconsin-produced food from the Cookery's menu.

Downtown Fish Creek can get congested in July, but you can escape the madding crowd in *Mr. Helsinki*, located just above the Fish Creek Market. This contemporary, art gallery/restaurant is a visual and gastronomical delight. Like the organic wine on the menu, Mr. Helsinki promises simple and seasonal dinner choices that feature grass-fed beef from De Pere, sustainably caught Alaskan salmon, greens from a Jacksonport organic farm, Wisconsin artisan cheeses, and an eclectic assortment of largely Asian-influenced entrees. Carnivores, vegetarians, and vegans will all feel at home here.

The Cookery in Fish Creek came back stronger than ever after a devastating fire in 2008. Now one the greenest businesses on the Door Peninsula, it supports Wisconsin farmers, just one of its sustainable practices. (photo by Pat Dillon)

In Sister Bay you can dine with a sunset view if you reserve a table early enough. The *Waterfront* is known for its hand-rolled pasta dishes and its dedication to using local farm ingredients on a seasonal menu. But the real treat may be in snagging a waterfront table and watching the sun set over Green Bay, a 180-degree backdrop. Its world-trained and -traveled chef will prepare vegan, vegetarian, or any other special request.

## Local Foraging

*Greens N Grains* in downtown Egg Harbor is chock-full of organic greens and meats, locally grown and raised. It also has many not-so-local organic grains and other natural products. A Travel Green Wisconsin–certified market, this sweet little grocery store is run by the same people who grow the local produce found in its coolers, Kathy Navis and her partner, Carmon Mabrey. With Navis behind the counter and Mabrey in his Jacksonport organic garden, this part of Door County offers an outlet for sustainable living and travel. Navis also runs a yoga and meditation studio called Junction Center and dedicates a small retail space in Greens N Grains

## Farmers' Markets

Door County is a labyrinth of orchards and privately owned farm markets. For a map to help you navigate the maze, download a brochure from the Door County Visitor Bureau's website (www.doorcounty.com).

Weekly farmers' markets that sell local fruit and produce from a number of area farms, plus crafts by area artisans, can be found at the following locations:

- Jacksonport Farmers' Market at Lakeside Park, Tuesday, 9 am to 1 pm
- Settlement Shops Farmers' Market in Fish Creek, Wednesday, 10 am to 2 pm
- Corner of the Past Farmers' Market in Sister Bay, Saturday, 8 am to noon.

to goods that support many sustainable practices. With the help of Navis and Mabrey, Egg Harbor launches guests not only onto the peninsula but into a sustainable foundation for peace-of-mind seekers and environmentally responsible travels.

*Harbor Ridge Winery*, on the southern end of Egg Harbor, houses a cafe, an art gallery, and a compound of local merchants who have adopted the healthy and natural, local and seasonal philosophy. This is a central location for art, coffee, lunch and dinner, locally made soap, artisan cheeses, and wine, and it houses a great kayaking outfitter (see What to Do). It is also a hub for the young Door County college and bohemian crowd, many of them seasonal workers, who support its live music venue. The winery has hosted sustainability workshops and events that have included the Thursday night "Art of Music at the Outpost" and a Sunday night "Meet and Greet the Artists" series coinciding with performances at the Peg Egan Performing Arts Center (see What to Do), an amphitheater in downtown Egg Harbor that holds free Sunday night concerts.

With no shortage of shops in Door County selling outsourced, manufactured goods, *EcoDoor* is a diamond in the rough, offering home furnishings made by local artists or from repurposed or recycled contents.

The Seaquist family is the largest tart cherry grower in Door County. They farm fifty acres of sweet and tart orchards along with some apples, raspberries, apricots, and pears. The Seaquists use the sustainable method of insect control integrated pest management (IPM), a research-based system using techniques that closely monitor conditions that surround the orchards, such as weather temperature, larvae counts, soil, and fruit tissue samples. And only when conditions that breed pests are evident do they apply pesticides, reducing application by 60 to 70 percent over the conventional method of routine calendar spraying. Jim Seaquist, who runs the business with his wife, Robin, his father, Dale, and Dale's wife, Kristin, educates groups about his methods for a small fee. Jim says other fruit growers in the Door County area are adopting IPM at different levels. You can go to the *Seaquist Orchards*, on Highway 42 between Ellison Bay and Sister Bay, for a first-hand explanation of how this works, or just go to their on-site farm market for the Seaquist family's fruit. This may be the greenest fruit in Door County.

## What to Do

From June to August, Egg Harbor's Harbor View Park hosts *Concerts in the Park*, sponsored by local businesses. Every Thursday you can enjoy a variety of musical genres, from jazz to blues to pop to bluegrass. View the schedule at the Egg Harbor Visitor Center's website (www.eggharbordoorcounty.org).

Egg Harbor is not without its performing arts events and the *Peg Egan Performing Arts Center* located at the Eames Cherry View Park is a big fish in a small pond. Their Sunday evening concert series is the product of two generous family giftings: Kevin Egan gifted the funds to create the performing arts center in the name of his mother, who was a passionate art patron, and the six-acre site of the Eames Cherry View Park was gifted by the Eames family of Egg Harbor with a stipulation that five acres remain planted with cherries.

The *Door County Trolley Premier Wine Tour* visits some of the peninsula's best family-owned orchards. It will take you to four boutique wineries, starting at the *Orchard Country Winery and Market* in Fish Creek, a fourth-generation family-run orchard that's as much about the Montmorency cherry and its products as it is about the wine it produces. Here you can get freshly packaged fruit or a still warm, home-baked pie, and you can taste their sweet cherry and fruit wines. Other stops are at Simon Creek Winery, Door Peninsula Winery, and Red Oak Winery. The tour includes a gourmet lunch at the Board Room at Liberty Square.

Other trolley tours include a narrated scenic tour of bluffs and the countryside and a culinary heritage tour of regional cuisine that includes stops at a European bakery, the locally owned Fisherman's Village, and gourmet markets.

Any territory surrounded by water has to have a lighthouse or two or, in Door County's case, ten. You can take a self-guided tour of *Door County Lighthouses*, arranged by the Door County Lighthouse Inn. The tour includes *Lighthouses of Door County*, a publication that includes a routing map to the lighthouses; tickets into Cana Island Lighthouse and Tower (accessible by a rock causeway); Eagle Bluff Lighthouses; and the Door County Maritime Museum in Sturgeon Bay.

Just south of the village, off Highway 42, is the *Ephraim Wetlands Preserve*, where you can hike through seven acres of swamps, marshes, bogs, flood plains, seeps, and wet meadows. This wetland is an important habitat for sixty types of wildflowers and numerous varieties of dragonflies, including the endangered Hine's emerald. It's interesting to note that the world's largest breeding population of Hine's emeralds exists in Door County, making it a destination for researchers from around the world. Look for this dragonfly's distinctive green eyes.

Even before you enter the *Ridges Sanctuary*, located east of Highway 57 on County Road Q north of downtown Baileys Harbor, it isn't hard to imagine what will unfold once you've entered the mulched trail. A wetlandenveloped, spring-fed stream percolates at the northern edge of the parking lot. This is just a precursor to a 1,440-acre boreal forest and wetland that stands distinctly apart from the nearby farm and residential landscape. Take the five-mile trail for a small fee; the sight of two Hine's emerald dragonflies attached at the tail is more common here than anywhere else in the world. Among the peat bogs and wet swales live twenty-five species of orchids, the locations of which are kept top secret unless you're carrying the right credentials. But birding is for everyone. View warblers of many types, from the common pine to the rare Canadian. Be sure to bring your field glasses.

You can download a Bicycle and Other Silent Sports brochure from the Door County Visitor Bureau's website (www.doorcounty.com) or pick it up from a location that best suits your activity of choice. Throughout the peninsula, there are five state parks and more than 250 miles of shoreline. Each park has trails for biking, hiking, and cross-country skiing and offers its own perspective of lake, dune, and forest, with an amazing array of vegetation and wildlife. You can rent a bike or scooter at *Edge of Park* in *Peninsula State Park* in Fish Creek, a Travel Green Wisconsin–certified park, or ride yours to *Newport State Park* located northeast of Ellison Bay (you can rent one there, too). You can also rent a bike in Fish Creek at *Nor Door*

*Sport and Cycle* and traverse the countryside on relatively flat and easy on-road routes between Highways 42 and 57.

*Potawatomi State Park*, a Travel Green Wisconsin–certified park named for the Native Americans who lived along Green Bay before European settlers arrived, is northwest of Sturgeon Bay and features the Run Wild event in October, a 10K run and fundraiser for the park sponsored by *Friends of Potawatomi State Park*. They have funded and placed Leopold Benches throughout the park, sponsor naturalist programs and candlelight skiing, and support the park's amphitheater. *Whitefish Dunes State Park*, northeast of Sturgeon Bay, features programs, exhibits, and brochures on archeology highlighting the importance of eight significant Native American villages listed on the National Register of Historic Places. *Rock Island State Park*, another Travel Green Wisconsin–certified park, is on primitive Rock Island and is two ferry rides off the northern tip of the peninsula.

Always wanted to be a lighthouse keeper? Join the *Friends of Rock Island State Park* to volunteer as a live-in docent for a week in the historic Pottawatomie Lighthouse on Rock Island. No cars, no bikes, no electricity, no running water, gorgeous views, and lots of fun. Green voluntourism at its best.

The guides at *Door County Kayak Tours* in Fish Creek like what they do a lot, whether it's handing out life jackets, hats, and sunglasses or giving a crash course in kayak safety. These tours are led by water-savvy college students with more energy than the riptide marked outside Whitefish Dunes Park, one of several locations kayakers are bused to, depending upon the winds and the weather. At the shoreline you'll get trained in kayaking etiquette and survival, and then you're on your own to paddle the lake with the group and experience mini-adventures along the way, such as circling the caves at Whitefish Dunes State Park. This tour is a one-way paddle with the wind, ending with a van pick-up. They promote "Leave No Trace" rules.

More kayak tours/rental and bike and winter sports-gear rental through-out Door County can be accessed at the *Kayaking Adventures Shop* in Egg Harbor, Nor Door Sport and Cycle in Fish Creek, Travel Green Wisconsin–certified *Bay Shore Outdoor Store* in Sister Bay, and *Ephraim Kayak Center* in Ephraim.

*Annual Events*

Look for the Ridges Sanctuary's *Door County Festival of Nature* schedule in April so you can book a program or two in May when tourist crowds are

## Get the Gear

This shop is housed in an old town hall on Highway 42 between Ephraim and Sister Bay. If you aren't watchful, you might zip right past. But if you're looking for something to augment any silent sport venture, *Ecology Sports*, a Travel Green Wisconsin–certified shop, is the go-to spot. Here you'll find everything designed to get you into nature comfortably and naturally. Or to read about it. Owners Marty and Nancy Drury run an outfitter gear shop on the main level and the Base Camp Cafe downstairs. They say their philosophy is "to support sustainable agriculture, environmental causes, and fair trade practices as they strive toward a world that is safe and clean for everyone's children." Marty is knowledgeable and convincing when he talks about the benefits of the Norwegian walking stick or other methods to help traverse the many Door County trails. He also promotes classes that originate at his shop that'll teach you the Drurys' mission.

down, prairie flowers are up, and migrating birds are moving through. This program includes guided field trips that focus on the Door Peninsula's biodiversity with a generous array of naturalist options. One takes you to the top of the Potawatomi State Park's observation tower and down to the park's sea caves. You can hike glacial drainage paths, explore wildflowers, watch wildlife in Anderson Pond, even write about it or sketch your visual experience. You can paddle waterways, bird with the experts, and attend programs on renewable energy. And when the sun sets, owls, frogs, and bats come out for observation.

In July, the *Peninsula School of Art* hosts the *Door County Plein Air Festival*, which attracts hundreds of painters and art lovers from across the country. The artists have six days to capture the landscape on canvas before the festival ends with the sale of their work at the school's gallery and at a live auction. That week painters can be seen along roadsides, tucked into the rock escarpment, and standing in fields and along the shorelines with easels and palettes and Tilley hats, often with awestruck crowds looking on. The school also offers premium-quality workshops and events all year-round that cover the entire arts spectrum. Many take you throughout the peninsula to paint, sketch, or photograph its myriad of amazing land- and seascapes. Its instructors are working artists from across the country as well as locals such as oil painter Lori Beringer from Plymouth and watercolorist Kari Anderson from Door County.

Go Run and Recycle at the *Door County Half Marathon* and *Nicolet Bay 5K* held in the month of May at Peninsula State Park. The half marathon takes runners along a U.S. Track and Field–certified paved surface within the park while the 5K starts at a different point but ends at the same finish line. Bring your old running shoes and donate them to the Go Run and Recycle program, which will send them to Wipers Recycling in Minnesota who turn rubber soles into absorbent materials used to clean up oil spills. The program is partnered with Door County's locally owned recycling service, Going Garbage and Recycling, one of several spots where shoes can be dropped off for recycling for a limited time.

## Local Arts

Next door to The Cookery is *TR Pottery*, another Travel Green Wisconsin–certified business and friend to the green movement in Door County. It is owned and operated by potters Tony and Renee Gebauer, who both left jobs as educators for the love of making pottery and have never looked back. Their work is well worth stopping to see: smooth, simply designed, functional bowls, cups, vases, vessels, and plates. Ever aware of their environmental impact, the Gebauers use innovative sustainable practices, such as giving pottery shards to mosaic artists and schools, not using printed materials, using waste heat from the kiln to heat the studio space in winter, and recycling wastewater and clay trimmings. Their good business practices are reflected in the simplicity and beauty of their work.

With an art gallery around every corner, it's truly hard to decide which one is worth hitting the brakes for. *Edgewood Orchard Galleries* is definitely one. More resembling a vineyard in Aix-en-Provence than a gallery tucked off Highway 42 in northeastern Wisconsin, Edgewood Orchard uses the natural landscape as its greatest canvas and the work of Wisconsin artists as its palette. With an outside sculpture garden and sitting area, this gallery is full of natural beauty, both inside and out.

*Gloria Hardiman* is a weaver whose shop is as much a piece of art as the hand-woven textiles she creates there. Located on County Road F, a stretch of road just outside Fish Creek said to be the prettiest in Door County, Gloria produces soft, artful garments in a space that is exploding with the same color and creativity that go into her work.

## The Cliffs of Door County

The Niagara Escarpment is a stretch of dolomite formation—you may know it as the limestone-like cliffs in Peninsula State Park or White Fish Bay Dunes State Park that follow the state along the Lake Michigan shoreline, for example. The escarpment is made by sediment deposited under inland seas more than 425 million years ago. It starts in New York, where it forms a deep gorge at the Niagara Falls, then travels southwest through Michigan and Wisconsin, and ends in northern Illinois. Recently it has been cited for its many rare microhabitats—crustaceans, snails, and delicate ferns and flowers. As it turns out, you don't have to leave Wisconsin for that perfect Niagara Falls honeymoon after all. But why would you want to leave Wisconsin, anyway?

Farther north, you'll find *Clay Bay Pottery* in Ellison Bay, a pottery studio and gallery set on a little hill that looks like a place to come home to for the holidays. Owners Jeanne and David Aurelius not only create functional pieces with whimsical folk art images of natural settings, like apple orchards and lakefront harbors dotted with sailboats, but they take their talents around the state as artists-in-residence, creating murals from images designed by schoolchildren. You can see their murals at scores of elementary schools from Fish Creek to Appleton to Milwaukee. Or you can stop at their gallery and pick up a bowl made with the same creative spirit. You can even go into their studio and watch potters at work.

If it's the performing arts that'll make your trip perfect, Door County has no shortage of opportunities. You could spend the summer basking in entertainment and never leave the peninsula. *American Folklore Theatre, Birch Creek Music Performance Center, Door Community Auditorium, Door Shakespeare, Isadoora Theatre Company, Midsummer's Music,* the *Peninsula Music Festival, Peninsula Players,* and *Third Avenue Playhouse*—the show goes on and on and on!

On the tip of the Door Peninsula, Jens Jensen (1860–1951) turned his amazing summer retreat into a serene getaway for people needing renewal from the stress of life within the Midwest's fast-developing cities. Jensen was a Danish landscape architect who worked in Chicago with Frank Lloyd Wright, among others. He made his mark in his field for being among the

## Protecting Door County's Natural Areas

Door County's Green Fund (www.greenfund.com) protects its environment through the works and support of people and businesses that contribute to this collective land effort. This private, nonprofit organization awards grants for land preservation and acquisition to permanently protect Door County's natural areas. The largest contributors to this fund are local businesses who understand the connection between protecting their natural environment and the tourist-driven economy that sustains them.

A group of local designers and furniture retailers came together and formed the Door County Furniture Guild to annually donate a portion of their profit on a designated day during peak tourist season. Check out the Green Fund website to see a list of those businesses and when best to patronize them, and for the extensive list of businesses that are regular contributors to this important environmental effort.

first to use native plants and natural settings, which can be seen throughout many of the Chicago parks that he designed. It was 1935 when Jensen founded *The Clearing*, what he called "a folk school." He was seventy-five at the time, but better late than never, and much better for Door County. His amazing stone architecture sits on a cliff overlooking Green Bay on 130 acres. Classes focus on mindfulness, both indoors and outdoors. Workshops allow travelers to attend for a few days, while others can participate in week-long resident programs. The Clearing's method of teaching is what the Danes call the living word: "Discussion, conversation, nature study, and hands-on work are emphasized, rather than learning just in the classroom, through reading and writing." The long list of classes includes opportunities to explore painting, quilting, writing, and literature. When classes are not in session, the Clearing offers two-hour tours of the historic site. Check its website for programs and for tour days and hours.

# Chequamegon-Nicolet Forest, Wisconsin's National Treasure

## Eagle River and Presque Isle Area

If trees could speak
They wouldn't, only hum some low
Green note, roll their pinecones
Down the empty streets and blame it,
With a shrug, on the cold wind.

—DORIANNE LAUZ, from "The Life of Trees"

Long before there was the snowmobile there was the snowshoe, worn by indigenous North Americans when thigh-high snowfall blinded pathways to their productivity. Eagle River, now the Snowmobile Capital of the World, is northwest of the 657,000 acres that is the Nicolet side of the Chequamegon-Nicolet National Forest. And to the southeast there's another 225,000 acres that is the Northern Highland–American Legion State Forest. The snowshoe is still used to traverse these northern woods, but now it's less about hunting and gathering and more about recreating. In winter months, the Eagle River area is a web of marked trails that are groomed specifically for snowshoers and cross-country skiers. In summer months, the trails are open for hikers and bikers. Waterways are plentiful and have become a haven for canoeists, kayakers, and other motorless sports enthusiasts. In addition, the forest management industry is rich with environmental outreach that puts you in the center of this delicate and endlessly stunning Northwoods ecosystem.

Compared with Bayfield County, the Vilas County hospitality industry trails behind in the getting-green business. While nature and wildlife conservationists abound to protect wetlands and promote responsible forest and wildlife management, lodges with a mission to promote conservation practices are few. But the ones that do are run by people who encourage travelers to tread lightly on the land as they enjoy the amazing northern Wisconsin landscape.

If you want to experience the Northwoods as its local people do, but prefer the Native American's perspective, the Lac du Flambeau area is your spot. Unfortunately, restaurants that focus on local, seasonal, and sustainable are few, owing to the lack of agricultural production in this part of the state. This might be the trip for staying somewhere that lets you call the shots in the kitchen—unless you stay in Presque Isle.

## Where to Stay

Marcy Chuckel manages *Lake Forest Resort and Club* in Eagle River as if the kitchens were her own and the cleaning products came from under her own sink. The staff mixes up batches of homemade air freshener, soft scrub, window-surface cleaner, ant powder, and deer spray, all so earth-friendly guests can buff-shine the kids with them.

Chuckel's mindset stands to reason. Lake Forest Resort sits on the outskirts of the pristine Chequamegon-Nicolet National Forest. Keeping chemicals out and bringing earth-friendly practices in helps Wisconsin's Northwoods retain its rich ecodiversity in this tourism hot spot that's vulnerable to overuse.

This "environmentally concerned" vacation spot, a Travel Green Wisconsin–certified resort, is dedicated to providing a place for tourists to enjoy one of Wisconsin's greenest playgrounds while teaching responsible land stewardship through its environmentally friendly business practices, as well as through community outreach. While each of the twenty-four townhouse condo units has a wood-burning fireplace, guests are asked to supply their own wood. The units overlook shimmering Voyageur Lake, one of the twenty-eight lakes in the Chain o' Lakes labyrinth that links itself right down to New Orleans via the Mississippi River.

Lake Forest Resort is set on 1,100 feet of lake frontage that is easily

At Lake Forest Resort in Eagle River, guests have access to nature trails and canoes to see the nest of an eagle that's been a longtime resident on Voyageur Lake. (photo by Pat Dillon)

accessed from each unit, with a sweet and simple nature trail that identifies indigenous trees and plants along the shoreline. And, if the shortage of restaurants in the area that focus on sustainable ingredients makes North-woods travel more challenging as you work to reduce your own carbon trail, Lake Forest condos provide a full kitchen for guests to prepare their own meals. You can find local specialty foods in the resort store.

One hour north of Eagle River you'll find the *Alpine Resort* in the little town of Presque Isle. Its owners are eco-visionaries Kim and Tim Bowler, who lead by example. Kim's enthusiasm for living the clean life in the Northwoods stems from a longstanding environmental awareness, but keeping it clean for her daughter, Cameil, is her priority. It was wishing to live where the water is pristine and lichen grows freely that prompted Kim and Tim to leave their day jobs in the Chicago area and move to Presque Isle, where they operate this Wisconsin Travel Green–certified resort on

The bridge at Lake Forest Resort lets guests look down into the crystal clear waters of Voyageur Lake. (photo by Pat Dillon)

Van Vliet Lake. Located fifteen miles north of Lac du Flambeau and thirty miles straight west of Land O' Lakes, the Alpine Resort is a vintage Northwoods experience with a present-day mentality. As their commitment to sustainable living, the Bowlers provide a chemical-free environment for their daughter and for their guests.

Cleaning products are eco-friendly, and erosion along the banks of their lake property is minimized with biologs that stabilize native species planted between them so they can root and thrive. If you check into one of their nine charming log cabins or one of five hotel units, you have access to canoes, kayaks, and paddle boats. If you bring your own boat, you're quickly informed about sustainable lake practices, such as keeping your boat clear of invasive species, like Eurasian milfoil and zebra mussels, two lake predators that are slow to invade this Northwoods area because of great land stewards like the Bowlers.

Kim and Tim Bowler maintain their Van Vliet Lake shoreline with biologs that stabilize native species planted between them so they can root and thrive. (photo courtesy of Alpine Resort)

And in the kitchen of this American Plan resort, one of the few remaining in Wisconsin, the food is as local and sustainable as Kim is able to provide. Eating organic has long been a way of life for this family, so providing it for her resort guests keeps her foraging for local suppliers, like her regular grass-fed beef grower and a local organic farmer. The Bowlers also grow their own herbs and spices and some tomato varieties on their chemical-free site. In winter, strap on snowshoes provided by the Alpine Resort and step outside for some of the best winter walks around. This resort is an oldie but green goodie.

Trees are one of Wisconsin's strongest and most plentiful natural and renewable resources. *Trees for Tomorrow*, just outside downtown Eagle River, was established to ensure that it stays that way. As the ultimate environmental outreach geared toward families, school groups, and lone travelers—it's even part of the National Elderhostel program—Trees for Tomorrow offers courses on the ecology of the northern forest ecosystem. Simply designed,

### Leave No Trace Rules

- Plan ahead and prepare.
- Travel and camp on durable surfaces.
- Dispose of waste properly.
- Leave what you find.
- Minimize campfire impacts.
- Respect wildlife.
- Be Considerate of other visitors.

this specialty school was founded as a forest restoration project by local paper and electric companies in the 1940s. Today it is on the National Register of Historic Places and caters to thousands seeking natural resource information.

Its self-guided walking tour of indigenous plants and wildlife is user friendly for travelers who are just passing through and want to simultaneously stretch their legs and their ecology knowledge. For groups and individuals who make this an overnight destination, Trees for Tomorrow has two dormitories that the staff describes as "modern rustic" with twelve rooms, four classrooms, and a dining hall that provides three squares and can accommodate vegetarians, vegans, and any other specialty foodies. Its programming provides conservation-based field workshops that teach sustainability and respect for our natural world.

Trees for Tomorrow also offers summer day camps for kids and programming that can be attended for a dollar. It gives a wide range of information about the ecosystem, from frogs to phenology (the study of how seasonal change influences the natural world, such as mammals emerging from hibernation, bird migrations, and flowers blooming) to salamanders to loons.

On summer nights, Trees for Tomorrow's public programming (free, but donations are accepted) covers topics important to understanding sustainability in the region, such as Wildlife Diseases, Leave No Trace camping, composting methods, and navigating with a GPS. This is environmental outreach designed with truly something for everyone. And since Trees for Tomorrow got its start by planting trees to save the Northwoods from logging and overburned areas, it will ship tree seedlings to you for one dollar each, with the proceeds benefiting Trees for Tomorrow school programs.

## Where to Eat

Fine field-to-fork dining is almost nonexistent in this part of the Northwoods, but Eagle River's *Riverstone Restaurant and Tavern* is trying. Located in a historic building along the Eagle River, a tributary of the Wisconsin River, the Riverstone offers artisan breads served with organic Wisconsin butter, Hook's and Pleasant Ridge Reserve artisan Wisconsin cheeses, organic spring greens, wild-caught Alaskan salmon, Wisconsin-made sausages, and Wisconsin microbrewed ales. With many restaurants in the area sticking to indigenous products like rice and cranberries, the Riverstone Restaurant and Tavern has definitely reached beyond.

## Local Foraging

*Grass Roots Health Foods* is an uncommon sighting in the Northwoods. You might notice the wind turbine before you notice the more common pine structure tucked up in the woods along Highway 70 near Lake Forest Resort, but once you've located the spot it's unmistakable. This is the go-to shop for locally grown produce (wild rice, honey, maple syrup) and nationally marketed organic goods, like tea and ginseng. And renewable energy—a wind turbine and solar photovoltaic tiles generate most of its power. Customers can get a full tutorial on alternative energy use and health food options. Take a notebook.

## What to Do

Lake Forest Resort activities focus away from motorized sports and onto family interaction. Guests can cruise Voyageur Lake in a canoe or kayak, or sign up for such atypical Northwoods activities as greeting card folding, T-shirt painting, and fitness walks through the recreation area. Friday nights, the couch potatoes are invited to the lounge for a free movie and popcorn.

The *Anvil National Recreation Trail* is one of the oldest and most popular areas for hiking and mountain biking in the Chequamegon-Nicolet Forest. In the winter months you can cross-country ski, snowshoe, and snow skate. It's also a designated area for observing wildlife and for birding. The Nicolet North Trail connects to the Anvil Lake Trail from the southeast along the Butternut Trail for another fifteen miles of cross-country skiing, hiking, and mountain biking. To reach these trails, drive 8.5 miles east of

Eagle River on Highway 70 to Parking Lot No. 1, or turn south on Military Road.

The *Three Eagle Trail*, a bike and hike trail between Eagle River and Three Lakes, is part of a larger plan to connect existing statewide trails. It is an 8.5-mile pathway with a ten-foot-wide crushed limestone surface. To connect the trail, take Sundstein Road south from Eagle River for a low-traffic, on-road four-mile ride through the town of Lincoln. The 8.5-mile limestone trail then goes through a quite, remote area before entering a stretch of woodlands and wetlands. Then it heads south down the Chicago and Northwestern right-of-way before ending at the Don Burnside Park in Three Lakes. From Three Lakes, you can access twenty-eight interconnecting lakes—the largest inland chain of freshwater lakes in the world—covering 7,626 acres.

The annual *Nicolet Wheel-A-Way* is a September event in Three Lakes that takes bikers through the scenic Chequamegon-Nicolet National Forest as a way to connect them with the forest's breathtaking vistas and its wildlife habitats. The noncompetitive event is designed for cyclists of all abilities. It's based at Don Burnside Park.

If you like the wilderness, some call the *Turtle-Flambeau Flowage* the Boundary Waters of Wisconsin. It's located about twenty miles southwest of Presque Isle near the town of Mercer, the Loon Capital of Wisconsin. Because of its isolated and rustic nature, it is highly recommended that an outfitter (see sidebar) accompany you on your first trip out, since this area is not for the faint of heart.

The 1926 construction of a dam to power a paper company created a reservoir that is more than 19,000 acres of water and 212 miles of shoreline. The area covers nine lakes, three rivers, including the Flambeau River, and several creeks. It's also known for its abundance of loons, known to nest only two to a lake. Loons and are becoming scarcer as their habitat becomes more compromised.

The flowage is a favorite among campers who like to rough it, with sixty remote but well-marked campsites set within this wild and rugged territory. If you're a thrill seeker, there is a twenty-six-mile Flambeau River canoe route that begins at the flowage and ends at the city of Park Falls. On this trip you'll negotiate twenty-three Class 1 and 2 white-water rapids and scores of waterfalls. This area is said to have some of the most spectacular displays of wildlife, from foxes and otters to the highest number of eagles, loons, and osprey in the state.

### Things to Remember to Help Protect Loons

- Respect slow/no wake zones and rules.
- Don't fish next to a loon.
- Use nonlead fishing tackle.
- Check your boat for aquatic invasive species.
- Leave native vegetation and woody debris on the shore and in the water.
- Use four-stroke motors or no motors at all.
- Spread the word.

A popular canoe route is the *Manitowish River Trail* that begins outside the town named for the spirit people of the Ojibwe, or "manitous." You can access the river at the origin of the Manitowish River, at High Lake off of County Road B east of Presque Isle. Or you can take a shorter, twenty-mile canoe route northwest of the flowage at Manitowish Waters. This trail starts at the Highway 51 bridge in Manitowish Waters and ends at Murry's Landing in Manitowish just outside Mercer, where you then have the option of accessing the Turtle-Flambeau Flowage. There are scores of river trails to paddle once you enter the flowage. For other routes and a detailed map of the rivers and the kind of terrain to expect, get the map *Rivers through Time: Canoe and Kayak Routes of Iron River, Wisconsin*, through the Mercer Chamber of Commerce (www.mercercc.com).

According to the Turtle-Flambeau Flowage website, you do need to exercise caution. The flowage has an abundance of stumps, logs, and rock bars. Water levels continue to be raised or lowered to benefit downstream hydroelectric plants. Even if you think you know your way around these changing water levels, you must slow way down in some areas.

If you brought the dog, the *Catherine Wolter Wilderness Area* is pet friendly and even allows dogs to run off-leash from August 2 to March 31. (April through July is reserved for ground-nesting birds.) A Nature Conservancy–protected area located between Presque Isle and Boulder Junction, this natural area occupies 2,189 acres within the Northern Highland–American Legion State Forest. Its fifteen lakes are surrounded by forest, native plants, and wildlife. You can carry in a nonmotorized boat, hike, cross-country ski

### Get the Gear and a Guide

If you're in the town of Three Lakes and need a kayak, or even a bike, call or go to *Three Lakes Do It Best Hardware*. This is a friendly, small-town hardware store that will deliver your gear anywhere you need it for three dollars a mile.

In the early 1970s, Dave Pucci drove five hours north to buy two canoes for his modest outfitter business in Eagle River. Instead, he purchased twenty-two at a bargain price. Soon after, while driving to work, Dave saw a three-acre parcel for sale on the Wisconsin River, bought it, and the *Hawk's Nest Canoe Outfitters* was born. He and his wife, Susan, both teachers at the time, haven't looked back. Today Hawk's Nest Canoe Outfitters owns 125 canoes and loads of kayaks across three locations: Eagle River (on the Wisconsin River), Manitowish Waters (on the Rainbow River), and Lake Tomahawk (near the Wisconsin River). Check out their website for on-site campsites, a complete list of outfitting provisions, a multitude of day and night river adventures, a shuttle service schedule, and rates.

In the Mercer area, *Rugger's Landing* is located on Pike Lake where the Turtle River runs through headed to Lake of the Falls and then into the Turtle-Flambeau Flowage. This is where you can rent a canoe, kayak, or tube and get help planning a trip that's geared to your time or skill level. You can also rent a cabin or cottage and bring along your well-behaved family dog.

and snowshoe, and do it all with Rover in tow. Trail markers and You Are Here signs will keep you directed.

A more adventurous outing can be found at *Guido Rahr Sr. Tenderfoot Forest Reserve*, another Nature Conservancy–protected site, five miles east of the Wolter area. To access it, you'll have to paddle Palmer Lake for approximately one hour. Once there you'll find a thousand acres of forests—five hundred of which are never-been-cut, old-growth forest—and two wild lakes, Mirror Lake and Roach Lake. To access it, launch your canoe at the Palmer Lake Boat Launch and paddle northwest across Palmer Lake to the Ontonagon River until the river hits Tenderfoot Lake. At the Conservancy dock on the northwest side of Tenderfoot Lake, you'll find the trailhead into the forest reserve. Follow the 2.5-mile loop to see old-growth forests and wild lakes, and if you still have the energy, follow a loop around

Mirror Lake for an additional mile of trail. The trails are well marked with arrow markers and You Are Here signs.

## Local Arts

Debra Ketchum Jircik's holistic lifestyle is central to her Eagle River *Circle of Life Studio and Gallery*. Once the site of a Northwoods resort built in the 1940s, it is situated on 4.5 acres on the shores of Meta Lake. Debra uses one of the original cabins as a woodshop and another as a summer gallery for her work and that of other like-minded artists. Debra, a UW–Extension master gardener, also works in a fifteen-year-old, fully equipped ceramics and papermaking studio where she teaches papermaking workshops for people of all levels. Her ceramic folk art representations of women are influenced by her Northwoods surroundings—women holding birds' nests and swans, wearing loons as hats. Her work often incorporates found objects as her way to recycle, such as cookie sheets and vintage flatware on her clay birdhouses. Debra works surrounded not only by the rural landscape, but by her organic gardens and a grotto and stone labyrinth that she built. People go here to be inspired by her art, her gardens, and her peaceful surroundings.

In July and October, the Eagle River area hosts the *Northwoods Art Tour*. Some of northern Wisconsin's best artists and artist-owned galleries open their doors to anyone interested in a behind-the-scenes look. The tour includes demonstrations and access to not-always-accessible studios. You can also purchase the artists' work.

There are historical museums and then there is the *Vilas County Historical Museum* in Sayner. It's a real Northwoods surprise. Set kitty-corner from where the first patented snowmobile was invented, the museum is just one fascinating collection after another, an enormous compendium of local artifacts that provide visual Vilas County storytelling. There is an amazing collection of Native American functional and decorative ware as well as two somewhat mind-boggling exhibits—one of taxidermied African wildlife and another of songbirds, many that are protected species, from all over the world. The story goes that the local hunter's court-ordered punishment for hunting illegally was to donate his collection. This museum was the only winner in that deal. There's tons more to see. Take the kids.

The town of Lac du Flambeau, or Lake of the Torches, named for the Ojibwe tradition of fishing by torchlight, is located in the Lac du Flambeau reservation northwest of Eagle River. With a population of three thousand, this reservation is home to the largest Native American group never to be forcibly removed from their territory. They proudly educate non-Native Americans about their culture through a number of well-respected venues. The *George W. Brown Jr. Ojibwe Museum and Cultural Center*, which houses the largest collection of Ojibwe artifacts, is one. *Waswagoning*, a twenty-acre re-creation of an Ojibwe village along Moving Cloud Lake, is another. This is an impressive reenactment of the Ojibwe heritage through traditional village activities. You can enter trail-connected birchbark lodges to watch Ojibwe members dressed in traditional regalia demonstrate such cultural traditions as birchbark canoe building, wigwam making, and dancing. In early spring you can get in on *ininatig*, the harvesting of maple syrup. A little later in the season, visit *Golden Eagle Farms* to pick organically grown strawberries.

Bring your bike to cruise Lac du Flambeau's quiet and scenic roads that run adjacent to and over numerous lakes, rivers, and wetlands. Two favored routes begin in downtown Lac du Flambeau and wind through the surrounding lake country. The first loop follows the shore of Flambeau Lake. The second loop is around Pokegama Lake, a picture postcard setting that includes views of other area lakes. And because the main roads are lightly traveled, biking to nearby Boulder Junction, Manitowish Waters, and Price County is manageable with those classic Northwoods, pine-tunneled views.

# Wisconsin's Waterfall Capital

## *Marinette and Langlade Counties*

The river has taught me to listen; you will learn from it, too. The river knows everything; one can learn everything from it. You have already learned from the river that it is good to strive downwards, to sink, to seek the depths.

—HERMAN HESSE, *Siddhartha*

Few places in Wisconsin have as much drama associated with their name as Marinette County. The residents claim that it, and its county seat, Marinette, are named for Marie Antoinette Chevalier, the daughter of a Menominee princess and a fur trader. Locals call her, affectionately, Queen Marinette. Whether or not they all believe that she was royalty, they do agree she was a shrewd businesswoman who ran a successful trading post with her three children after two husbands abandoned her. But the real drama surrounding this area is the landscape and its water resources. Marinette County alone boasts more than twenty cascading waterfalls, thus crowning it Waterfall Capital of Wisconsin. And Marinette and Langlade Counties both have a plethora of placid to powerful rivers, like the National Wild and Scenic Wolf River and the Peshtigo River. Along these waterways you can take your pick of outfitters who'll drop you off and pick you up downstream (or up, if you're a real glutton for punishment). In White Lake, there is an adventure resort that you can check into that'll take you paddling along the Wolf River and the Menominee Indian Reservation and won't bring you back until you know the difference between running a drop and a shallow slide. Unless you insist. If you'd like to add some cultural and historical perspective on how the Native Americans came to the area and gain some insight into their sustainable agricultural practices, take a detour to the Oneida Nation around Green Bay. Since the slow food movement has yet to creep into this area's culinary mainstream, you might have to settle for tried and true family-owned restaurants that feed the local economy.

## Getting There

Langlade is fifty-eight miles from Peshtigo, a stop on the *Indian Trails* bus line between Hancock, Michigan, and Milwaukee (with connections to Chicago). Boxed bicycles may be checked under the coach for a fee.

## Where to Stay

When you spend your days running hair-raising Class 3 white-water rapids carving across waters federally designated as "wild" and spinning in sticky holes and keepers, you aren't going to let an F4-class tornado bully you. Even if it wipes out your resort, escapes with your trees, and brings your livelihood to a screeching halt.

In the summer of 2007, this scenario played out at the *Bear Paw Outdoor Adventure Resort* two miles from the Wolf River in White Lake, in the southeast corner of Langlade County, just over the Marinette County line. A tornado hit the ground running for forty miles, taking out almost everything in its path. By fall, with little left but determination and a loyal staff, resort workers, neighbors, and repeat guests, owner Jamee Peters joined forces with her programming director, Scott Berry, and began a long, arduous cleanup and restoration of the devastated site. Jamee considers the out-pouring of help that eventually got Bear Paw back on its feet to be an even more overwhelming experience than having watched the tornado advance from the window of her walkout basement.

By the spring of 2008, the Bear Paw was back in business with a regular schedule of canoe and kayak clinics to accompany its six new pine cabins, two pine chalet units, ten ridge-side campsites, and four rustic cabins. But Jamee wasn't about to stop there. By June 2008, she had the Bear Paw Pub up and running as well as the Gear Shop, the only gear shop north of Minneapolis that sells white-water kayaks.

This show of fortitude just might be the best recommendation this resort has for its canoe and kayak clinics and classes, since Bear Paw's primary

## DNR Carry-in Firewood Rule

To protect parks and forests from firewood pests, the Wisconsin DNR has created a permanent rule that prohibits bringing firewood onto any DNR property from more than fifty miles away or from outside of Wisconsin.

function is as an adventure resort. Situated on 25 acres of land that Jamee owns, and another 250 acres of private and publicly owned land that she uses, the Bear Paw's tornado-torn hiking, biking, and cross-country ski trails are being newly forged, including trails that lead down to the Wolf River. You can stay at the resort and forgo a clinic or class, but then you'll have to bring your own canoe or kayak. Bear Paw rents no canoes and rents kayaks only to guests who have taken a class that teaches the fundamentals of paddling a rough riverway. Clinics and classes run from April to October, when Bear Paw Pub and the Gear Shop close. Lodging is available all year.

Forty miles northeast of White Lake is the little town of Silver Cliff where you can camp alongside the Peshtigo River. At *Kosir's Rapid Rafts*, a popular white-water rafting outfitter in Marinette County, you can camp just steps away from the river and then take one of its Class 3 and 4 rapid-rafting trips in the morning. The spring trip is chilly but the water is fast and high, so beginners should not sign up. Summer trips are bit calmer but the ride varies with the weather, so come prepared. Next door at *Rapids Resort* you can rent a simple cabin with a full kitchen that overlooks the river.

If you'd like to camp where you can hear the rush of a waterfall, go to *Twelve Foot Falls Park*, nineteen miles north of Silver Cliff in the town of Dunbar on the Pike River. This is remote tent camping that puts you in the center of Marinette County's waterfalls tour (see What to Do). Lily Lake is nearby for swimming. The falls are located just west of Highway 141, off of Highway 8. Go south on Lily Lake Road and follow the signs to Twelve Foot Falls Road. This is a county park, so a fee will apply.

### Where to Eat

Seventeen miles east of White Lake in Mountain lives Amy Donaldson, a Biro Culinary School graduate who wanted to share her love of cooking in her idyllic, wooded country setting. Her *Amy's at Woodhaven* is a kitchen with a U-shaped bar that seats fourteen participants for interactive cooking

Amy Donaldson prepares a culinary feast using herbs from her own garden and locally grown ingredients from the Kellner Back Acre Garden in Denmark. Donaldson offers cooking workshops out of her home in Mountain in Langlade County. (photo courtesy of Amy Donaldson)

classes with a focus on sustainable ingredients. Along with group-taught dinners, Amy offers relaxation and nature retreats that include massage, yoga, meditation, and hikes. She also works in conjunction with Spur of the Moment Ranch, south of Mountain. If your group just wants a lovely place to gather, Amy will cook you up a sustainable feast. She gets her eggs, chicken, beef, lamb, and pork from Red Bank Farm in Suring, where they proudly say they treat their poultry like royalty. Amy also harvests from her own organic garden and raises free-range chickens that yield eggs for her daughter Ellie to collect and sell at markets around town. Amy also uses local sources for raspberries, honey, and maple syrup. She's not kidding around when she claims to serve truly "green" cuisine.

Okay, these restaurants won't sustain much beyond a local economy, but we can't overlook that part of sustainability when the rest hasn't arrived. The *Bear Paw Pub* is said to have the healthiest food in the Langlade–White Lake area. Jamee Peters never uses canned ingredients and is known for her great homemade pizza. If you're touring waterfalls near Crivitz, go to the

## Arugula, Corn, and Tomato Salad with Shaved Parmesan, from Amy's at Woodhaven

Arugula, also known as rocket, is a small, spicy green with a peppery flavor. You can do this salad with other greens, but the peppery taste of the arugula plays well against the sweetness of the corn and tomatoes.

1 1/2 cups (lightly packed) fresh basil leaves, torn
1 1/2 cups corn kernels (cut from about two small ears)
1 cup halved cherry tomatoes
3 tablespoons olive oil
2 tablespoons fresh lemon juice
6 cups (lightly packed) fresh arugula (about 4 ounces), or mixed greens
2-ounce piece parmesan cheese.

Whisk oil and lemon juice in small bowl. Season to taste with salt and pepper. Toss with corn and tomatoes and let stand for about 30 minutes. Then divide salad greens (arugula) among plates and top with corn and tomatoes. Using a vegetable peeler, shave curls of parmesan atop each salad and serve. Makes 4 to 6 servings.

---

*Pines Supper Club.* It's a Northwoods supper club known for pizza it makes from scratch. If you happen to be paddling the Peshtigo River where it exits at Green Bay near Marinette, get in line (it's a popular spot) at *Mickey-Lu Bar-B-Q*, a locally owned diner that's been in Marinette for decades. This authentic 1950s diner remains unchanged by time and technology. Wash down a cheeseburger with a chocolate malt and you've done Mickey-Lu's the way the locals do it. Eat there or take out. A local favorite in Peshtigo is *Schussler's Supper Club*, which serves German fare with homemade dumplings, spaetzle, and other specialties.

### Local Foraging

Visit the Oneida Nation on your way up to Langlade and Marinette Counties. It is off the beaten path but well worth the trip. This displaced tribe settled in the western Great Lakes in 1822 after the Oneida Warriors found their homeland in New York confiscated by the British settlers after

This eagle welcomes visitors to the Oneida Nation outside Green Bay as it stands proudly over reservation monuments that memorialize its fallen soldiers. (photo by Pat Dillon)

the Revolutionary War. Along with other migrating tribes, the Oneida people struggled to keep their land in Wisconsin after taxation laws rendered them unable to pay up to fraudulent land companies. It wasn't until the 1930s that 1,270 acres were placed in trust for the Oneida Nation. Learn about their heritage through tours of the *Oneida Museum*, pow-wows, and storytelling. And visit their community-supported organic farm, *Tsyunhehkwa* (joon-henk-qwa), which means, in a broad sense, life sustenance. This agricultural community has a mission to reintroduce high quality, organically grown foods that will provide a healthier and higher quality of life. The farm runs twenty acres of rotational crops, twenty-five acres of grass-fed cows, a solar greenhouse for herbs, and a berry garden. It also raises white corn, hay, pumpkins, fruits, and vegetables.

---

**Dried Sweet Corn Soup, from Oneida Nation, the Powless Crew**

This soup is served at Oneida ceremonies, sweats, and traditional feasts.

1 pound of dried kidney beans
6 potatoes cubed
$^1/_2$ pound of side pork or salt pork, cubed
1 pound dried venison or dried beef
4 cups of dried sweet corn
about one gallon of water; if corn expands too much, add more

Boil corn, kidney beans, and pork for one hour. Add dried meat and potatoes. Cook about one more hour or until everything is done.

---

While you're there, you can visit the pick-your-own *Oneida Apple Orchard*, which uses a sustainable integrated pest management process to reduce the use of chemical pesticides. You can also get the Oneida Nation's canned products, organic produce, and other Native American herbs, arts, and crafts at *Tsyunhehkwa Natural Retail Store* and the *Oneida Farmers' Market*, at the Oneida One-Stop at the intersection of Highway 54 and Seminary Road. The Oneida Nation encourages you to visit *Oneida Nation Farms*, west of Highway 41 off Highway 54 just west of Green Bay.

*Pleasant View Orchard* in Niagara is named for its vista of the amazing Menominee River valley. A family-run outfit, Pleasant View Orchard yields high quality apples for local markets and sells homemade pies and maple syrup on-site.

On your way to the Oneida Nation, you can stop at the *Kellner Back Acre Garden* in Denmark to purchase pasture-raised chickens, turkeys, and eggs. The Kellners also grow flowers and herbs and harvest honey on-site. All are available for purchase. Call ahead for a farm tour.

## What to Do

The Menominee Indian Tribe is indigenous to Wisconsin. Their five ancestral clans—bear, eagle, wolf, moose, and crane—originated at the mouth of the Menominee River as far back as ten thousand years. By the

### Farmers' Markets

- *Crivitz Farmers' Market*: Saturdays from 8 a.m. to noon, mid-August through mid-October. At the Green Thumb Garden Shoppe on County Road A in Crivitz.
- *Green Bay Farmers' Market*: Saturdays from 7 a.m. to noon, June through October. At the parking lot between Cherry and Pine Streets in Green Bay.
- *Green Bay West Festival Foods Farmer Market*: Mondays from 7 a.m. to noon, July through mid-October. 2250 West Mason Street in Green Bay.
- *Green Bay East Side Festival Foods Farmer Market*: Wednesdays from 7 a.m. to noon, July through mid-October. 3534 Steffen Court in Green Bay.
- *Marinette Farmers Market*: Tuesdays and Fridays from 7 a.m. to noon, June through October. Main and Wells Streets in Marinette.

early nineteenth century the tribe occupied ten million acres of what is now Wisconsin, Michigan, and Illinois. Today, due to a series of U.S. government treaties, including the Menominee Termination Act, which removed federal recognition of the tribe, they occupy as few as 235,000 acres forty-five miles northwest of Green Bay in Keshena. You can visit the *Menominee Indian Cultural Museum* to learn more about this indigenous tribe and how they won back their recognition and hung onto their cultural identity. You can also take a white-water raft trip on the Wolf River through the reservation's *Shotgun Eddy*, an outfitter located seventeen miles north of Keshena on Highway 55.

Marinette County is the Waterfalls Capital of Wisconsin, with ten falls scattered among its twenty county parks. Many waterfalls are easily accessible from *Marinette County Parks* parking lots. Go to the Crivitz Recreation Association's website (www.crivitzrecreation.com/falls.html) and print out a complete walking tour that has each waterfall destination, a photo of the falls, and a detailed description of what your walk will entail. But Marinette County knows that there's a lot to see and more ground to cover, so it has created four mini-tours. Each is a self-tour of two or more falls within close proximity, which makes seeing a variety of waterfalls in a day doable. Go to http://therealnorth.com/waterfalls for descriptions of the four tour options. About half of the waterfalls on these tours are in the Marinette County

Park System, so there is a fee. Pack a lunch and get out there; you might be able to cover more falling waters in one day than the county thinks you can (it recommends two or three days). Don't forget the camera!

The Peshtigo River has multiple personalities. With some of the most difficult white-water rapids in the Midwest running above Caldron Falls Reservoir in the Chequamegon-Nicolet National Forest, extreme sports athletes get a double whammy adventure—amazing white-water rush through a spectacular forested sideshow. The slower, wider side runs below the town of Crivitz and is for the more leisurely paddler who wants to take the panoramic view in stride. The central river reservoirs create a balance, with flowage that accommodates all paddling abilities and degrees of skill. This ride calls for a life jacket and a waterproof camera.

Paddle the *Peshtigo River State Forest*'s twenty-five miles of river and 3,200 acres of flowage, or hike or cross-country ski its 9,200 acres of rustic forest. Wisconsin's newest state forest, it borders Governor Thompson State Park, another recent acquisition. There are fifteen access points along the river. Contact the Peshtigo River State Forest headquarters in Governor Thompson State Park for information on boat landings.

*Thunder Mountain County Park* is the highest point in Marinette County. This 160-acre park includes hiking trails and Thunder Mountain Overlook, which provides spectacular views of western Marinette County, including High Falls Flowage. It is said to have the best mountain biking in the area and great hiking. Follow County Road W west from Crivitz for 14 miles to Cauldron Falls Road, then north 2.5 miles, then west on Thunder Mountain Road. In September, the annual Peshtigo River Trail Paddle and Tour leads canoeists and kayakers down lower Peshtigo River with a guide and discussion about history and natural features.

# Enter, Northwoods

## Rhinelander Area

Only to the white man was nature a wilderness.

—LUTHER STANDING BEAR (1868 –1939), Lakota Chief

Rhinelander greets northbound travelers just southwest of the Chequamegon-Nicolet Forest. This town claims the centrally located confluence of the Wisconsin and Pelican Rivers, once a base for the Sioux Indians until European loggers edged them out to take over land for sawmills in the late nineteenth century. Today the 230 lakes lying within a ten-mile radius provide unlimited tourist opportunity. And with Rhinelander's mission to turn itself into a more "walkable and bikable" community for locals and visitors, many paths lead to these lakes, while many more are in the development stage.

While the area is still a mecca for snowmobilers in winter months, the Northwoods has a growing number of local advocates for sports activities that are lighter on the land and kinder to the air. Many of its business proprietors have been of the tread-lightly mindset long before the green travel trend.

### Where to Stay

A likely scenario at *Holiday Acres* in Rhinelander on any summer day might have Kim Zambon hosting a breakfast cookout surrounded by horses from the Holiday Acres stables and families who have come back to a pine cabin on Lake Thompson year after year. Or, one might find Kari Zambon tending her Turn of the Century boutique inside a century-old log homestead that's

The Zambon family has preserved the cabins on Lake Thompson so that Holiday Acres has the same family-oriented feel it had when Kim Zambon's parents were at the helm. (photo by Pat Dillon)

filled with not-your-everyday Northwoods resort wear but clothing made from sustainable materials, alongside beeswax and Himalayan salt candles. And then there's Max, the resort golden retriever, who greets guests as they check in. Your well-behaved canine companion is also welcome here.

This resort is simple. It's a Wisconsin original that's Travel Green Wisconsin–certified. It has pine log walls with oil paintings by Kim's sister Chris Zambon, a Los Angeles artist who interprets these wooded surroundings in swaths of bright, expressive colors rather than the traditional Northwoods palette. The Zambons are the third in this fourth-generation, family-run resort founded by Kim's grandparents over sixty years ago, which is why treading lightly on the land that they love is taken very seriously. And always has been.

You won't find photovoltaic tiles glinting off the tops of their vintage pine cabins or a wind turbine generating clean energy, but you will find

In the 1970s, this century-old building was relocated from the site of the first resort owned by the Zambon family's great-grandmother. Kari Zambon now uses it to house her Turn of the Century gift shop at Holiday Acres. (photo by Pat Dillon)

a clean, simple resort that harkens back to the day of the now defunct American Plan vacation, still catering to simple-living seekers as its core value. The grounds are graced with games families play together: tennis, volleyball, and shuffleboard. Cabins are filled with nothing disposable besides the requisite toilet paper and a single soap wrapper. And while their Three Coins Restaurant has yet to jump on the green cuisine bandwagon, Kari Zambon, a cookbook collector and the primary menu designer, will proudly direct you to those items that have trickled down the recipe chain through these four generations, such as Kim's grandmother's oat bread, still served in a basket alongside her dill bread. Full cabin kitchens provide an opportunity for travelers preferring an organic diet to bring their own food supplies and prepare their own meals. Each cabin is equipped with a recycling bin, an uncommon sight in the Northwoods.

## Gramma Hazel's Oat Bread

Served Fridays at Holiday Acres Resort.

$1/4$ cup melted butter
4 cups oatmeal
1 quart warm water
1 cup brown sugar
2 tablespoons salt
$2 1/2$ tablespoons yeast (regular)

Mix all ingredients. Allow the mixture to work until it begins to be bubbly. If you prefer, proof the yeast in some of the warm water with a bit of sugar before adding other ingredients. Gradually add 6+ cups flour until it is smooth. Place on a well-floured surface and knead in about $1 1/2$ cups additional flour, or more, until moderately stiff, smooth, and elastic. Kneading is good exercise! Place in a large buttered or oiled bowl and turn to grease all surfaces. Cover. Allow dough to rise in a warm place until doubled. It may not rise quickly, so allow enough time and do not rush it. It may be $1 1/2$ hours. Gently deflate, divide in four, and shape into four loaves. Place in greased 8 by 4 or 9 by 5 pans. Cover and allow to raise again until doubled. Spray lightly with water and sprinkle with loose oatmeal to decorate loaf. Bake at 350 degrees for 35 to 40 minutes, or until they are quite brown. Allow loaves to cool completely before slicing. Four $1 1/2$-pound loaves.

While silent sports activities like canoeing, kayaking, and rowing are available and encouraged (the Zambons conduct thorough "clean water, clean boat" checks on visiting boats), the Zambons host a not-so-silent but completely earth-friendly sport of sorts each spring. It is the annual Jazz Festival and Jazz Camp, run by the Zambons' brother-in-law Kim Richmond (Chris's husband), a Los Angeles musician, composer, and University of Southern California adjunct professor. The faculty consists of musicians from around the country, some Wisconsin born or based.

Holiday Acres has a wide sweep in good, family-oriented recreation and entertainment, a healthy, happy place to drift in a canoe, paddle a kayak, and kick up the jams.

## Where to Eat

The Northwoods isn't the green cuisine center of the universe, but it has a few under-the-radar merchants selling organic and sustainable products as a lifestyle rather than a gimmick. *Golden Harvest* is one of them. Owners Timothy and Nicole Conjurski believe that good food production doesn't process the nutritional value from its ingredients. Here you'll find organic bulk grains, dried fruits and berries, and Wisconsin-grown organic produce and dairy in a grocery store–like format. All bakery is Golden Harvest–made and starts with chemical-free Montana-grown whole wheat and fruit that's raw—apples are peeled for pies and blueberries are frozen for use in off-growing seasons. Their garden center sells organic gardening products. Conjurski has even convinced some local growers to go green.

The *Country Seed*, just a few blocks west, takes a little different approach to natural food. Here you can get not-so-local everything, from alpaca-wool mittens knit in India to natural pet products, natural skin care, and vitamins. Locally, the Country Seed brings in organic Amish-grown produce from Granton and free-range, grass-fed beef from Gilman. Between the two stores, most natural food and product needs will not go unmet.

There's one green fast-food alternative and it's a dandy. *Joe's Pasty Shop* is a small, locally owned, Travel Green Wisconsin–certified business with a picnic-style charm to its simple decor. Owners Larry and Jessica Lapachin use innovative green business practices, like recycled papers and wax paper instead of plastic, and purchase carbon credits to offset their own carbon emissions. But the real bonus for hungry travelers is their delicious, traditional pasty recipes that use organic meats and locally grown products. They are as delicious as their makers are friendly and happy to serve them up.

## Local Foraging

Rhinelander's *Hodag Farmers' Market* sells vegetables, crafts, local specialties, organic food, and fruits. On Saturdays from June to October it's located at Pioneer Park by the Logging Museum.

## What to Do

Use the cleanest of energy by biking or hiking Long Lake Nature Trail, a fifteen-minute walk from Holiday Acres Resort. The trail, set on a small glaciated lake, is partially covered with a floating bog and is home to moisture-loving trees and plant life, like white birch, moss, and lichen in the uplands, and black spruce and tamarack in the lowlands. See if you can locate the less common plants, like winterberry and Labrador tea and red pitcher plants. If you want a guided tour, sign up for one of Holiday Acres Resort's naturalist programs offered on Sunday afternoons from mid-June until mid-August. Each week a Trees for Tomorrow naturalist has a thousand acres on which to illustrate the Northwoods' diverse ecosystem while heightening awareness and respect for the land.

You'll find art with a heart if you follow Highway 47 north for ten miles out of Rhinelander to McNaughton. There you'll see the sign that directs you to the *Riverrun Center for the Arts*, a Wisconsin Travel Green–certified art gallery slightly off the beaten path. Owner and potter Joan Slack, a passionate through-the-arts historian, doesn't just spin functional ceramic pieces out of the gallery she built on family land she escaped to as a child. She also spins stories from clay by replicating pottery designs of the Paleolithic people who evolved into the Lakota and Ojibwe tribes, the Native American ancestors who once inhabited the land on which Slack works. Long interested in the concept of "place," Slack reveals in her work a deep understanding of what she calls the many "layers and lives that have existed in the Northwoods." Also a wool felter using wool she gathers in Scotland and Ireland, Slack learned her technique while researching the prehistoric, Celtic, and monastic arts in Ireland, her ancestral home to which she now conducts tours focusing on Irish traditions. With her own layers of archeological interest and her love of the land, Slack takes these dimensions into her classes and workshops. Some focus on prehistoric artists and potters, while others take students into the northern forest for inspiration. She also offers local tours that introduce tourists to Northwoods artists and historic sites, such as sacred Indian burial grounds, while connecting people with the lore of the land.

*Nicolet Area Technical College*, a Rhinelander green centerpiece, gets high marks not just for its management of more than two hundred acres of sylvan land and its thousand feet of frontage along the pristine shores of Lake Julia, but for being Wisconsin's college campus leader in renewable energy use. But its commitment to sustainability goes beyond its renewable energy center, which boasts two photovoltaic tiles and a wind turbine, produces clean energy for the campus, and is used in the teaching curriculum. It also provides outreach education on the positive impact of tapping into the state's renewable energy systems and on private installation.

It also educates the community about the state's Clean Boats/Clean Water campaign as part of the Lake Julia Stewardship Project, which promotes the health of the lake through ecosystem studies.

To the locals and travelers, the Nicolet technical college is also fertile ground for summer outdoor adventure with its nature-based programs that explore Wisconsin's and Upper Michigan's rich biodiversity with paddling trips into the wilderness of the Upper Peninsula and hikes that study the diverse flora and fauna of the Northwoods. There is even programming that offers yoga, sauna, and brunch in the wild. These courses are all taught by individuals who have stories that tie them impressively to the land for which they advocate.

About thirty minutes southeast of Rhinelander is the *Sokaogon Chippewa Community*, a 1,700-acre reservation in Mole Lake known historically for the Battle of Mole Lake in 1806 when five hundred Sokaogan and Sioux clan members died in a clash over ownership of the rice fields. More recently it's known for a battle to keep metallic-sulfide mining off the Wolf River. In October 2003, the Mole Lake Chippewa (Ojibwe), who settled among the rice beds of the Great Lakes region more than a thousand years ago, and Forest County Potawatomi Indian tribes won a thirty year fight to prevent metallic-sulfide mining off the Wolf River that was a direct environmental threat to wetlands, Ojibwe wild rice beds, Native burial sites, and prized fish in the Wolf River. This grassroots movement created allies between adversarial groups, such as sport fishing groups, environmentalists, rural residents, urban students, and unionists, and drove out the world's largest resource corporation and the world's largest mining company. As a result, a collaboration between these local groups and nonprofits, governments, businesses, and individuals are developing environmentally and culturally sustainable tourism opportunities along the Wolf River, including the Wolf River Scenic Byway Initiative, which seeks to have Highway 55 adjacent to the river become a state, and ultimately a national, scenic byway. Currently, every September, you can watch as tribal members ceremoniously harvest rice from nearby Rice Lake, one of three small lakes on the reservation. This is also the site of the historic Dinesen House, designated one of the ten most endangered properties in Wisconsin. Constructed in 1860, this log home was a respite for mail carriers on a military road between Fort Howard in Green Bay, Wisconsin, and Fort Wilkins in Copper Harbor, Michigan. It was later acquired by a Danish expat, Wilhelm Dinesen, who lived there with an Ojibwe housekeeper until he moved back to Denmark. His daughter, Karen Blixen, whose pen name was Isak Dinesen, wrote the book *Out of Africa*, which became a major motion picture.

*Bearskin-Hiawatha State Trail* is a multiuse trail of crushed red granite that supports primarily biking and hiking while crossing one of the densest concentrations of lakes in Wisconsin. Each trail runs along the former Milwaukee Road's Northwoods Hiawatha railbed from Minocqua and Tomahawk. The Bearskin runs south from Minocqua for 18.3 miles, and the Hiawatha runs north from Tomahawk for 6.2 miles and they meet at a six-mile break of ungroomed trail between Harshaw and Tomahawk. Designated a National Recreation Trail, it includes views of wetland birds and rolling, wooded hills. You can begin the trail from behind the Police Department in Minocqua and at the north side of the Sara Park Activity Center in Tomahawk.

# Quiet Waters

## *Waupaca Area*

A great blue heron owns this part of the river.

—ROBERT BENADA, innkeeper

The gently rolling glacial landscape west and south of Waupaca is dotted with clear kettle lakes, and State Natural Areas protect many acres of its varied ecosystems. North of Waupaca, the countryside is a patchwork of small fields traversed by narrow, lightly traveled roads. A segment of the Ice Age Trail meanders west of town, bisecting Hartman Creek State Park, where the park's lakes form quiet oases in the busy Chain O' Lakes. Wisconsin Rustic Road No. 23, a popular biking route, connects the park with Rural, a village on the National Register of Historic Places. When you think of the Waupaca area and the Chain O' Lakes, pontoon boats, water skis, and jet skis probably come to mind. But for the traveler seeking nonmotorized outdoor fun, this area has lots to offer. Bicycling, hiking, canoeing, cross-country skiing, snowshoeing, and nature watching are all popular pastimes. Locally grown foods fill the Waupaca Farmers' Market on Saturdays and are featured in two local eateries. And there's a lovely green bed-and-breakfast inn in Rural.

## Getting There

Waupaca is on the *Lamers* bus line's daily route between Milwaukee and Wausau.

## Where to Stay

The clear water of the Crystal River burbles gently through Rural, and the historic buildings of the *Crystal River Inn Bed and Breakfast* lie right along the stream. The 1853 A. R. Potts farmstead—home to Potts and his descendents for 120 years—has been a bed-and-breakfast since 1987. Helen Potts, who grew up in the house her grandfather built, lives down the road.

In 2005, Robert and Deborah Benada bought the inn and began an extensive program to improve bird and wildlife habitat on the property with several acres of prairie and woodland restoration and native plant landscaping. There's a small pond and a cattail minimarsh on the property. The National Wildlife Federation has certified the inn's eleven acres a wildlife habitat. The Benadas installed seven bluebird houses and monitor them for the Bluebird Restoration Association of Wisconsin, and at least fifteen bluebirds fledge each year. After only three years, they had identified fifty-eight species of birds on their property. In 2007, guests saw a yearling barred owl fall from a branch. Steve Hoffman from Hartman Creek State Park took the bird to Feather Rescue near New London. They released the healthy bird at the inn in late September.

Near a huge presettlement bur oak that still stands on the hill above the inn, Robert and Deb added a classical, seven-circuit, grass meditation labyrinth. Many of the outbuildings, like the restored 1902 dairy barn, are as old as the farmstead. They recycle containers as well as buildings, and they compost both yard waste and food waste for their vegetable and flower gardens.

The main building is a traditional B&B, with seven guest rooms and six common areas decorated in historic style. (The Benadas added their own touches with local art, including work by Charlotte Fung Miller, a Chinese brush artist from Mukwonago.) Secluded quarters are also available: a former chicken house became the smaller of two guesthouses. The larger cottage can be rented by two separate parties or combined to include a kitchen, sitting room, and loft and can sleep up to six people—an option which works well for families.

*Hartman Creek State Park's* campground has showers and flush toilets, and campers choose from sites in a red pine forest, a mix of old apple trees and hardwoods, or a remotely located tepee campsite. Some campsites are open all winter. The park's green initiatives include prairie restoration, invasive species control, and recycling programs.

Green innkeepers Robert and Deborah Benada serve tea by the Crystal River. (photo by Robert Diebel)

## BGBY Greenbirding (Self-propelled Birders Birding Locally)

On a tip from Wisconsin birder David Hamel of Westfield, we're passing along a challenge from some green Canadian birders:

"The Big Green Big Year (BGBY) is a low-key, friendly bit of birding rivalry that is not especially original but which seems appropriate in these days of carbon emissions and climate change. If you have ever felt even a tiny bit guilty about driving or flying to see a good bird (or several) why not join us in a year of carbon-neutral birding?

"The Big Green Big Year has the acronym BGBY and is therefore pronounced Bigby . . . and it is simply a Big Year in which you count only those species seen within walking or cycling distance *of your home or principal place of work.* As simple as that, no dashing off to the far corners of the planet burning fossil fuels as you go."

—Richard Gregson, Baie d'Urfé, Québec (www.sparroworks.ca)

## Where to Eat

As a guest at the Crystal River Inn, you'll enjoy a hearty breakfast. Fair trade, shade-grown, organic coffee and hot chocolate and homemade banana or pumpkin breads are laid out early. (Because of the impact nonorganic banana farms have on birdlife, the Benadas buy only organic bananas.) Then Robert and Deb serve a full breakfast in the Sun Room or Breakfast Room. When the bugs are behaving, you can also eat in the gazebo by the river. To spread on the great breads they bake, the couple preserves their own jellies and jams from local chokecherries, black cherries, and pin cherries, as well as wild grapes and wild plums that they gather, and four kinds of mint (including chocolate) that they grow in pots. Next to the 1902 dairy barn, they grow basil, potatoes, zucchini, yellow squash, rhubarb, and other vegetables. They buy local strawberries, local hydroponically grown tomatoes, and other produce from the farmers' market. Mrs. Peterson, right down the road, keeps them supplied with raspberries in season.

In the nearby historic hamlet of King, lunch at Sandi Schuettpelz's *Freckled Frogg* is a feast. Look for an improbably small white cottage along County Road QQ, just down the road from the Veterans Home, and a sign that is simply a wordless graphic of a leaping frog. It's open during warm weather only and reservations are necessary, so be sure to call ahead. Definitely order a salad. Sandi creates what many customers call works of art, the best salads they've ever eaten. The desserts are homemade from Sandi's family recipes. If you don't eat everything, Sandi will pack up your leftovers on a real plate—a friend hunts up garage sale plates for her—and send it home with you, to be returned after you finish your food. Almost all are returned, which Sandi calls a testament to her wonderful customers. Greens, edible flowers, and herbs come from Sandi's own pesticide-free garden, and raspberries, tomatoes, and other fruits and veggies from King Berry Farm (see below) down the road. Sandi uses local meats, eggs, and dairy as much as possible. According to Rob Walker in his recent book *Buying In*, it's all about connection and uniqueness. Sandi offers both.

On Waupaca's Main Street, the gourmet food at Bonni Miller's casual *Chez Marché Cafe* is a locavore's delight. Bonni's weekly menu follows the seasons. Starting in March, lettuces from a hoophouse in Nelsonville mean weeks of wonderful big salads. Main season veggies are grown by several local farms and in Bonni's home garden. In September, expect to find tomatoes popping up everywhere, including in a tasty grilled cheddar and

Sandi Schuettpelz, owner of the Freckled Frogg restaurant in King, is creative in the way she serves delightful lunches and runs her green business. (photo by Lynne Diebel)

tomato sandwich. Great Wisconsin cheeses like Pleasant Ridge Reserve and local cheddars and swiss cheeses from Star Dairy in Weyauwega are mainstays, as are eggs from a farm near Waupaca. The grass-fed beef for your burger comes from within five miles. When you stop here for lunch or dinner, don't expect fast food—leave time to savor the local flavors. Do expect a taste of local art—the works of the featured visual artist as well as occasional live music and poetry readings.

## Local Foraging

Après dining at Chez Marché, stop next door at *The Bookcellar*, an indie bookstore, to shop for new and used books, compact discs, LPs, cassette tapes, periodicals, and musical instrument accessories. And on the topic of books, during Waupaca Public Library's new *Waupaca Book Festival* in early October, you can attend readings by guest authors at various Waupaca venues, including Chez Marché. The 2010 author list included Jacquelyn Mitchard.

If you stay in the Crystal River Inn's Little House on the Prairie, you'll have a kitchen. And after a visit to the *Waupaca Farm Market* on the town square, you can cook locally sourced foods, everything from fruits, veggies, and flowers to syrup, honey, and grass-fed beef. The market is held daily in season, but Saturday's market is by far the best.

During the *Waupaca Strawberry Fest*, held the third full weekend in June, local growers sell huge numbers of their fresh strawberries (and strawberry shortcake) at stands in downtown Waupaca.

*King Berry Farm* sells its own veggies, fruits, honey, and jam at the farm store on King Road.

## What to Do

Definitely don't sit inside—the countryside calls. If you enjoy hiking, the *Ice Age Trail* is a good start. Yellow blazes on trees and yellow signs mark the trail. Start at Edminster Road and hike south into Hartman Creek State Park. When you finish the Faraway Valley loop, marked with green blazes, you will have logged over six miles.

If you start hiking at Stratton Lake Road and hike into the Emmons Creek Fishery and Wildlife Area, you'll find oak savanna in the *Emmons Creek Barrens State Natural Area*. Here wild lupine grows in thick stands, providing habitat for the Karner blue butterfly. Robert and Deb Benada of Crystal River Inn discovered that wild American plums grow along Emmons Creek Road. (Keep in mind that the fishery and wildlife area is open to hunting during the season.) When you finish your trek, there's a sandy swimming beach on the south side of Hartman Lake. The Ice Age Trail also runs north from Rural Road to Indian Valley Road.

In winter, the Ice Age Trail becomes, rather appropriately, a cross-country ski route. In Hartman Creek State Park, you'll find 6.8 miles of classic groomed and 2.2 miles of skate groomed cross-country trails and a shelter. Other trails in the park are designated for snowshoeing.

Bicycling along Wisconsin Rustic Road No. 23 from Rural to Hartman Creek Road is a lovely route, recommended in many guidebooks. In Hartman Creek State Park, you'll find about five miles of designated off-road bike trails, marked with signs, for which trail passes are required. Information on four area bike routes ranging from one to seven miles is available at the park visitor center.

From the little hamlet of King, the Wau-King Trail—a paved trail for hikers and bikers only—runs for 3.9 miles to Waupaca, where it connects with the River Ridge Trail.

### The Freckled Frogg's Secret Raspberry Vinaigrette

1 pint fresh-picked King Berry Farm raspberries
$^1/_3$ cup Jake's Local Clover Honey or My Sister Linda's Maple Syrup
half of one small red onion or shallot, minced
$^1/_3$ cup fine vinegar of your choice (don't be afraid to be creative)
$^1/_2$ cup canola oil (always add oil last in any vinaigrette and add very slowly
   for a nice, smooth dressing)

For a slightly different variation you may add any *one* of the following:
$^1/_4$ cup mayonnaise
$^1/_4$ cup crème fraîche
1 tablespoon Dijon mustard
sprig of fresh mint (rose petals or lavender are my favorites)

**Use:**
fresh ground white pepper
a pinch of sea salt

This dressing is a beautiful brilliant plum color! Note: I prefer to make my dressings a bit thicker and concentrate on the natural flavor of the featured fruit or vegetable in the recipe.

—Sandi Schuettpelz, The Freckled Frogg

With all the lakes and streams around Waupaca, canoeing and kayaking are natural choices for outings. Paddling the Crystal River from Rural to Shadow Lake Road takes you right past the Crystal River Inn. If you have a shallow draft canoe or kayak, you'll have fun running the riffles and light rapids of this crystal clear stream, dodging deadfalls, and cruising under multiple stone bridges. Launch your canoe or kayak at Main Street and Cleghorn Road in Rural (where you can get a twenty-five-cent ice cream cone at the *Weller Store*, a trip in itself). After three miles, portage around the Little Hope Mill Pond dam. End your four-mile adventure just upstream of the bridge at County Road K, by the *Old Red Mill*, a charming historic spot that's the site of many weddings.

Another possibility—for experienced river paddlers only—is a seven-mile voyage on the Waupaca River from County Road Q to Brainards Bridge

Park. There's a covered bridge along the way, and the trip ends in Class 1 rapids. Read Mike Svob's *Paddling Southern Wisconsin* for details.

In Hartman Creek State Park, paddlers enjoy a beautiful chain of four quiet lakes—Knight, Manomin, Pope, and Marl. (Knight Lake is connected to the others but outside the park.) Motorboats are allowed, but a no-wake rule slows them way down. Launch your canoe or kayak from the public access south of Golkes Road, at the end of Knight Lane. Shallow channels connect the crystal clear lakes. At Marl Lake, a stone staircase leads from the dock to the Whispering Pines picnic area.

For anglers, the Crystal River is a Class A trout stream, and native brook trout are caught in Radley Creek, south of Rural on Highway 22.

In the *Myklebust Lake State Natural Area* one mile south of Iola, a carry-in canoe landing gives you access to a twenty-acre lake. The lakeshore is completely undeveloped, and fishing for northern pike, largemouth bass, and panfish is said to be quite good.

### Local Arts

Lovers of local art should plan their visits during the *Arts on the Square* on Waupaca's town square in August. And during the *Hidden Studios Art Tour* in October, biking the Waupaca portions of the route is a green (and scenic) option.

# Where the Wisconsin River and Farmers Won't Be Ignored

## *Wausau and Stevens Point Area*

Local food is a handshake deal in a community gathering place.

—BARBARA KINGSOLVER, *Animal, Vegetable, Miracle*

When a national art magazine features the most "respected exhibition of bird art in the world," you add this cultural tidbit to your list of great reasons to put this town on your sustainable travel itinerary right alongside your birding agenda. But Wausau, the principal city of Marathon County, has many reasons to be on your list. Marathon is the largest county in the state, the Wisconsin River courses right down its center, and there are more than fifteen hundred square miles of vast wetlands with great birding. Ironically, it's the paper mill industry that has sunk resources into supporting, directly and indirectly, some of the area's most natural and spectacular attractions. These include more than 240 species of birds found collectively along the Eau Pleine River and Lake Du Bay, both of which are created by paper mill dams on the Wisconsin River. When you're there, take note of the scores of cars with kayaks strapped to their roofs. They're not there en masse by chance. With the Wisconsin River in its grip, Wausau is an international hub for canoe and kayak competitions on the world-class white-water rapids course that races through its downtown. Here you can learn to kayak cautiously or watch the experts navigate the rapids at break-neck speed.

And maybe the fact that Wausau lies near the crosshairs of the forty-fifth parallel and the ninetieth meridian, placing it at the center of the northern half of the Western Hemisphere, is more of an interesting geographic morsel than a green tourism draw, but it does add luster to the positioning of Rib Mountain, the fourth highest point in the state. From Rib Mountain you can access trails for every off-motor sport you can think of: cross-country and downhill skiing, snowshoeing, birding, hiking, biking, backpacking, even yodeling if you're so inclined. In downtown Wausau, an ice skating rink adds loads of charm to a thriving arts district while accentuating the joy of slowing down. Combine these attractions with one of the greenest inns in the state and the area's eat, buy, and stay-local availability and Wausau appeals in any season!

South of Wausau, the Stevens Point area sustains the land steward mentality. It's Wisconsin's seventeenth eco-municipality, a community that uses the Natural Step framework for developing its local environmental, social, and economic health. The Natural Step is a Swedish model that uses citizens and sectors of the larger community as a guide for the sustainability process. Stevens Point's natural resource–oriented university nurtures sustainable farms and businesses and restaurants. Look past the industrial smokestacks in the area, which speak to an age-old industry that has sustained this Northwoods economy for generations, and you'll see a new, more eco-conscious era. Out-of-towners may tend to bypass the Wausau area en route to the upper Northwoods, but for those who are inclined to stay central, good things await.

### Getting There

Stevens Point and Wausau are on the *Lamers* bus line from Milwaukee via Appleton. Boxed bicycles can be checked under the coach, and the boxes can be stored at the Wausau terminal. Wausau is also on the *Jefferson* line from Milwaukee to Minneapolis.

### Where to Stay

Paul and Jane Welter looked at thirty-five properties for their bed-and-breakfast before choosing the *Stewart Inn*, a George W. Maher–designed beauty in the heart of Wausau's Andrew Warren Historic District. With it came the original approval drawings presented to the Stewart family in the late nineteenth century, and later the Welters acquired nine original construction drawings done by Maher himself. So in the transformation, they were careful to restore, reclaim, then reuse, keeping all aspects of

Paul and Jane Welter preserved the interior of a historic mansion designed by George. W. Maher for their Stewart Inn, finding a new home for every architectural element removed during restoration. (photo courtesy of the Stewart Inn)

conservation in mind—both mindfulness for the earth and the integrity of Maher's architectural vision. Every cabinet, light fixture, sink, and trim piece that was removed has been reused elsewhere in the mansion. The five lovely guest rooms, all with original pieces of signed art, carry the names listed on the original blueprint.

This B&B, a Travel Green Wisconsin–certified inn, is not only lovely for its original architectural beauty and the Welters' conservation efforts, but it is conveniently located for walking or biking to wonderful events and attractions in downtown Wausau. These include the Arts Block, summer concerts on the city square, white-water kayak competitions, and the Leigh Yawkey Woodson Art Museum.

Staying in Stevens Point puts you central to a wide variety of attractions. If you're hiking the Ice Age Trail, *A Victorian Swan on Water* is a member of Friends of the Ice Age Trail and is Travel Green Wisconsin–certified. For a

**Green Bed and Breakfasts, Some with Ice Age Trail Shuttle Service**

Nearly fifty Wisconsin bed and breakfasts are Travel Green Wisconsin–certified, and several of them are located on or near the Ice Age Trail. For a small gratuity, some innkeepers will pick you up at or near the trail, shuttle you back to their inn, and return you to your trailhead the next day. For a complete list of Travel Green–certified inns, go to the Wisconsin Bed and Breakfast Association website (www.wbba.org/wisconsin-travel-green.php). For a list of inns located on or near an Ice Age Trail that may provide shuttle service, go to the Ice Age Trail website (www.iceagetrail.org/overnight-options).

---

small fee, owner Joan Ouellette will pick you up from the Ice Age Trail and make you feel at home in her classic Victorian home. Joan is happy to give recommendations about the area and serves up breakfasts of fresh fruit from the farmers' market, grass-fed meat from Raikowski's Farm in Junction City, and other natural foods. Then she'll take you back to the Ice Age Trail. You just might feel you've stayed with family. The Victorian Swan is located near the Stevens Point Brewery, which you can tour.

### Where to Eat

*Downtown Grocery*, a socially responsible, multifaceted grocery store, is the total green package. It is designed to offer local and other products to neighbors and office workers, giving them another option to live more sustainably. Here customers can buy produce, meats, dairy, and eggs from local, regional, and organic farmers and producers. Blaine Tornow of Moonshadow Farm and Kevin Korpela of ObservatoryDrive.com (an idea services firm that combines Korpela's expertise in design, community building, and sustainability) run this business partnership with a creative, friendly, and neighborhood-oriented vision. From its inception, Blaine and Kevin, a Wausau native who recently returned to practice architecture in his hometown, followed earth-friendly practices. For example, the storefront is located on a "main street," the historic interior space was restored, lumber from the deconstruction was reused, local lumber harvested from Moonshadow Farm was crafted into the store's interior furnishing, and earth-friendly finishes were applied to the walls, floors, and cabinetry.

Wausau's Downtown Grocery exhibits art by area children that reflects their notion of healthful food and community gardening. (photo by Pat Dillon)

Downtown Grocery is a full-service grocery store and an everyday farm market that includes a kitchen that prepares vegetarian fast food with a four-week rotating lunch. It's a limited but much-sought-after menu. All of the soups use made-from-scratch stocks. The store carries store-branded products, including Kombucha (a cultured Chinese tea), and pie crusts made without lard or partially hydrogenated oils. It also shares food ideas in cooking classes, offers tapas (Spanish-type appetizers) during the summer concert series, and fills its website (downtowngrocery.com) with food and store tidbits. And a real treat is the store's art gallery, where paintings, or "crops," created in local art classes feature themes relating to the store's vision of sustainability and food. The paintings are hung, or "planted," on the walls and new "crops" are "rotated" into the gallery with a public event, called a "crop rotation party."

Down the street, the *Back When Cafe* is housed in an extensively renovated historic space across the square from the Arts Block. As part of the slow food movement, this fine-dining restaurant places a premium on using local and fresh resources.

At Sentry Insurance headquarters, @1800 is a mecca for slow food lovers. This five-star eatery prepares dishes with indigenous and homegrown ingredients presented as inventively as contemporary dining gets. You might find stravecchio from Antigo or Highland beef from Columbus's Fountain Prairie Farm and Inn. Think globally, eat locally. Not cheap, but worth it. While you're there, be sure you take in the @1800 Gallery, which sometimes features the work of local artists right alongside a permanent collection of more recognizable names—Chagall, Picasso, Dine, Dali, and Calder—to name a few. No kidding.

Don't let the location of *Emy J's* fool you. The little strip mall–like building has a fair trade coffeehouse that blends smoothies with strictly fresh (but not local) fruit, yogurt, and honey from Iola, Wisconsin. It also serves sandwiches you can take to one of its wonderful mosaic-tiled tables made by none other than Emy J and her parents, owners Guy and Maria Janssen.

*Adventure 212* is a locally owned health club and spa with a restaurant, *Bistro 212*, that follows the field-to-fork philosophy. Its menu is loaded with items from local and organic farmers, many of whom they maintain a relationship with, so they're on the same page as to how their food is grown.

*CPS Cafe* is run by students and faculty of the Department of Health Promotion and Human Development at the University of Wisconsin–Stevens Point and is connected to sustainable family farms. Open Monday through Friday during the regular school year, it is located on the first floor of the College of Professional Studies Building. Check for hours.

## Local Foraging

On *Moonshadow Farm*, located just outside downtown Wausau, Downtown Grocery co-owner Blaine Tornow runs a Midwest Organic Service Association–certified organic farm that grows market vegetables and produces eggs available at Downtown Grocery and for a CSA program. The eighty-acre farm is in a pastoral setting and includes a rustic year-round rental cabin, called Hemlock Cabin, located next to a three-acre field of purple coneflowers in bloom from August to September. Blaine grew up around food, as his family once owned a large local grocery store. He also operates Tornow Forest Products, which supplied lumber for the cabinetry at Downtown Grocery.

The *Stevens Point Area Co-op* smacks of a corner grocery store, but it's better. It supports healthful, whole foods and environmental responsibility through the sale of holistic and local goods and the use of photovoltaic tiles to source solar energy. Its on-site bakery, *Earthcrust Bakery*, also uses clean energy and produces organic whole grain goods. The only downside is that you'll have to find your coffee elsewhere to go with your Earthcrust bakery purchase. Try Emy J's

*Mullins Cheese* in Mosinee, just west of Wausau, is the largest family-owned cheese factory in Wisconsin.

*Wisconsin Dairy State Cheese Company* is in Rudolph, just west of Wisconsin Rapids. Here, through a large observation window, you watch cheese curds being made, and you can go home with a complete assortment of Wisconsin-made cheeses.

Good Earth Farm is a co-op of six farms in the area around Milladore, located a few miles northwest of Stevens Point. Collectively they raise Belted Galloways and Cornish Cross hens, among other animals that live on grassland that is free of agrichemicals. The co-op is managed by *Gifts from the Good Earth Farm* owners Mike and Deb Hansen, who view the Milladore area as "an organic wasteland," which is why they work hard to nourish their land and animals. On their eighty-acre dairy farm they use an intensive rotational grazing system and work with the land and not against it. It's a great model for sustainable agriculture. The co-op's products are available online and can be shipped from their farms to your door. Or go to the Gifts from the Good Earth Farm, where the Hansens welcome visitors who call ahead.

*Stoney Acres Farms* is a third-generation farm in Athens, twenty-eight miles west of Wausau, where supporting a healthy and socially just world is central to its organic farming philosophy. The family grows vegetables, herbs, and fruit; makes maple syrup; and raises grass-fed beef and chickens. When you visit, they'll harvest products for you right on the spot.

Twenty-eight miles southeast of Wausau in Elderon is *Maplewood Garden*, where 170 varieties of chemical-free herbs, berries, and vegetables are grown and are available to anyone who stops in. Owner David Peterson also bottles up maple syrup, in the tradition of his grandfather who farmed the same land in the late nineteenth century. His specialty crop is gourmet garlic and shallots. For a reasonable fee, you can get an educational tour of the gardens and hear about Peterson's farming philosophy: learning how to feed people right and then feeding them.

## Connecting People to Their Food

The central Wisconsin people who make up *Central Rivers Farmshed* are committed to creating a renowned, local food community. Through Farmshed, local residents can stay connected to people who grow their food. It encourages participation through education, cooperation, and action in supporting its local food economy. Its website offers a list of Central Rivers Farmshed events in the Stevens Point area, such as the annual energy fair held each June in Custer or workshops that promote sustainable eating, such as how to can food, use root cellar storage, make applesauce, and freeze and dry food.

## What to Do

With the Wisconsin River running through the center of town, Wausau is the logical site for world-class white-water kayak and canoe competitions. The Wausau course at *Whitewater Park* in downtown Wausau combines a natural riverbed and vertical drop with dam-controlled water flow. It offers a consistent level of difficulty regardless of weather. Some people come to ride the rapids, others come as spectators. Either way, this city hosts scores of competitions and holds a variety of kayaking classes and adventures. Wausau's white-water program has been named a Center of Excellence by the United States Canoe and Kayak Team, making it a top training site. For descriptions and a calendar of events, competitions, and classes, go to Wausau Whitewater's website (www.wausauwhitewater.org).

The hill that *Rib Mountain State Park* sits on is a billion years old, making it an elder among the earth's geologic formations. At 1,940 feet above sea level, it's the fourth highest peak in the state, towering 760 feet above the open plain. Within its majestic 1,500 acres you can access a wide array of activities. Hike its 13.6 miles of hiking trails, of which 8.2 are accessible to people with disabilities. Snowshoers will find 8.2 miles of groomed trails for their sport. Climb to the top of the 60-foot lookout tower for an 800-foot overlook, or climb almost that high along many of the hill's rock wall embankments (climbers.com). You can ride the *Granite Peak Ski Hill* chairlifts before the snow falls for truly remarkable views, or come back in peak snow season and hit the downhill slopes—same incredible view, new ground cover.

Unrack your bike on the *Mountain Bay Bike Trail* trailhead in Weston, a township just six miles south of Wausau, and for four dollars a day you can take the trail east clear over to Green Bay, a "mere" eighty-three-mile trek. The trail follows the former Chicago & Northwestern right-of-way and intersects the Ice Age Trail in Marathon County, the Wiouwash Trail in Shawano County, and a number of trails in Brown County.

*Nine Mile Forest* is a heavily wooded forest with a trails system of 27-plus miles that includes 15.5 miles of cross-country ski and snowshoe trails and an eight-foot-wide skate-skiing lane. It offers a range of biking level challenges from May to September. Check into the *Wausau Wheelers* biking club for weekly guided mountain and road trips of varying levels of difficulty. Snowshoe and cross-country ski equipment rentals are available.

In Stevens Point, the 30.5-mile *Green Circle Trail* is a hiking and biking trail that actually makes a circle while it connects urban residents with secluded natural areas that surround the city. The trail has fourteen connecting segments and links Stevens Point's Bukolt, Zenoff, Pfiffner, Plover River, and Iverson Parks; Plover's Lake Pacawa Park; the Village of Whiting Park; the UW–Stevens Point Schmeeckle Reserve; and Izaak Walton League land.

Six miles from Stevens Point, the *George W. Mead Wildlife Area* is a study in biodiversity and conservation, starting with thirty thousand acres of wetlands, forests, and grasslands that boast 267 species of birds, including 193 that breed on the property and 19 known rare species. Its 6,208-square-foot education and administration facility exemplifies sustainable and environmentally responsible construction with five renewable systems in place: wind, photovoltaic, solar hot water, geothermal, and wood biomass. During its construction phase, many sustainable design measures diverted 95 percent of its construction waste from a landfill. From its website you can download guides to birding and maps on hiking and biking trails. Bring your canoe or kayak to paddle the Little Eau Pleine River and its surrounding wetlands.

Cranberries are Wisconsin's number one fruit crop. In fact, Wisconsin is the country's top cranberry-producing state and working to lead the industry in sustainable production. According to the Wisconsin State Cranberry Growers Association, growers have undertaken fifty-one environmental projects through the Natural Resources Conservation Service to conserve marsh water and put nutrient management plans in place. Some growers have worked with the U.S. Geological Survey to monitor loon nesting habits in central Wisconsin marshes.

Brian Ruesch of *Ruesch Century Farm* in Wisconsin Rapids is one of the very few growers to harvest his berries with the rakes used in the late nineteenth century. This method allows him to harvest without water, which causes less bruising and a longer storage life. He says it's a time-consuming process and inefficient, "back-breaking" work, but that it's the best process for the consumer. You can visit his farm and watch him harvest the old-fashioned way or pitch in as a volunteer. "My whole deal is that our society must remember the past in order to appreciate what we have," Ruesch says. "By harvesting this way people can appreciate the marvels of the modern machine and how America innovates, and it also reminds people of how difficult life was a century ago. Plus, customers win as they get a berry with a long-lasting shelf life along with new knowledge."

*Local Arts*

The *Performing Arts Foundation Artsblock* is named for the arts and theater district in downtown Wausau. It's devoted to cultural arts, thus supporting Wausau's title as the leading small arts community in the Midwest. The Grand Theater houses Wausau's performing arts community, which has thrived there for more than one hundred years, first with the Grand Opera House in 1899 and then in 1927 with the construction of the Grand Theater. Since then, the Grand has been Wausau's showplace for the arts, with a major renovation project in 1987. Later the facility was expanded to incorporate two historic office buildings on the block and new facilities, including the Great Hall and the Greenheck Lounge, an elegant skybox rental space overlooking the theater. The adjoining building houses the Caroline S. Mark Gallery and The Loft, both operated by the Center for Visual Arts. In winter months, you can ice skate directly across the street from the Grand Theater. And when the snow flies, this historic downtown is an idyllic winter setting. The Grand presents national shows, from Broadway musicals to popular culture revues. The Center for the Visual Arts is an impressive space with exhibitions featuring the fine art of local and regional artists in a range of media.

The art scene in Wausau isn't limited to the ArtsBlock. Just east of downtown, birds take flight in all media, starting with the Margaret Woodson Fisher Sculpture Garden that greets guests as they approach the entrance of *Leigh Yawkey Woodson Art Museum*. This 1931 Cotswold-style English Tudor was home to Alice Woodson Forestor, who donated the property in memory of Leigh Yawkey Woodson, her mother and a Wausau philanthropist, to be

Wildlife and nature are a central theme at the Leigh Yawkey Woodson Art Museum where the world-class Birds in Art exhibit is held each September. (photo by Pat Dillon)

Wausau's only art museum at the time. The museum's mission is simply to enhance lives through art. With exhibitions that include a wide range of art from around the world, the museum also has a commitment to art found in nature, as demonstrated through its internationally celebrated annual Birds in Art exhibit held in September. If you enter expecting to find bird art but come across the original storyboards from an internationally famous children's book author-illustrator, don't be surprised. The Leigh Yawkey Woodson Art Museum connects kids to art through this biennial exhibition of children's book illustrations. Past exhibits have included such well-known author-illustrators as Eric Carle and Paul O. Zelinsky.

# Resources

## Travel Green Wisconsin

Travel Green Wisconsin is a voluntary program run by the Wisconsin Department of Tourism that reviews, certifies, and recognizes tourism businesses and organizations that have made a commitment to reducing their environmental impact. Specifically, the program encourages participants to evaluate their operations, set goals, and take specific actions toward environmental, social, and economic sustainability. At the time this book was published, 267 businesses statewide were certified. The public can read evaluations of participating businesses on the program's website, www.travelwisconsin.com/wisconsin/Travel-Green/Overview.aspx.

## Great Green Reading

Anderson-Sannes, Barbara. *Alma on the Mississippi, 1849–1932.* Alma, WI: Historical Society, 1980.

Breckinridge, Suzanne, and Marjorie Snyder. *Wisconsin Herb Cookbook.* Madison: Prairie Oak Press, 1996.

Dott, Robert H., Jr., and John W. Attig. *Roadside Geology of Wisconsin.* Missoula, MT: Mountain Press, 2004.

Feldman, Stephen. *Fabled Land, Timeless River: Life along the Mississippi.* Chicago: Quadrangle Books, 1970.

Fremling, Calvin R. *Immortal River: The Upper Mississippi in Ancient and Modern Times.* Madison: University of Wisconsin Press, 2006.

Hembd, Jerry, Jody Padgham, and Jan Joannides, eds. *Renewing the Countryside: Wisconsin.* Minneapolis: Renewing the Countryside, 2007.

McLimans, David. *Gone Wild.* New York: Walker Publishing Company, 2006.

———. *Gone Fishing.* New York: Walker Publishing Company, 2008.

Rogers, Elizabeth, and Thomas M. Kostigen. *The Green Book: The Everyday Guide to Saving the Planet One Simple Step at a Time.* New York: Three Rivers Press, 2007.

Sibley, David Allen. *The Sibley Guide to Birds*. New York: Alfred A. Knopf, Chanticleer Press, 2000.

Svob, Mike. *Paddling Northern Wisconsin*. Rev. ed. Black Earth, WI: Trails Books, 2006.

———. *Paddling Southern Wisconsin*. Rev. ed. Black Earth, WI: Trails Books, 2006.

Trask, Crissy. *It's Easy Being Green: A Handbook for Earth-Friendly Living*. Layton, UT: Gibbs Smith, 2006.

## Periodicals and Booklets

*Birds in Art*, Leigh Hawkey Woodson Art Museum

*Ice Age Trail Companion Guide*, www.iceagetrail.org

*The Leopold Outlook*, www.aldoleopold.org

*The Places We Save: A Guide to the Nature Conservancy's Preserves in Wisconsin*, www.nature.org/wherewework/northamerica/states/wisconsin/preserves/art35.html

*Stories of Stewardship: Tales from Wisconsin's Big Backyard*, Gathering Waters Conservancy, www.gatheringwaters.com

*Northbound*, www.treesfortomorrow.com

*Sustainable Times*, www.sustainabletimes.net

*Wisconsin, Naturally: A Guide to 150 Great State Natural Areas* (includes a statewide map), www.dnr.wi.gov/org/land/er/sna

## Useful Websites

Central Rivers Farmshed, www.farmshed.org

Chequamegon Area Mountain Bike Association (CAMBA), www.cambatrails.org

Home Grown Wisconsin Cooperative, www.familyfarmed.org; www.cias.wisc.edu/crops-and-livestock/home-grown-wisconsin-marketing-fresh-produce-cooperatively

Land Stewardship Project, www.landstewardshipproject.org

Leave No Trace, www.leavenotrace.ca/programs/principles.html; www.wiparks.net

Local Harvest, www.localharvest.org

Natural Resources Foundation of Wisconsin, www.wisconservation.org

Saint Croix River Valley Buy Fresh Buy Local Chapter, www.dinefreshdinelocal.com

Wisconsin Association of Lakes, www.wisconsinlakes.org

Wisconsin Dairy Art Network, www.wisconsindairyartisan.org

Wisconsin Department of Natural Resources, www.dnr.state.wi.us

Wisconsin Environmental Initiative, www.wi-ei.org

Wisconsin Farm Fresh Atlases, www.farmfreshatlas.org

Wisconsin Local Food Network, www.wisconsinlocalfood.wetpaint.com

Wisconsin State Natural Areas, www.dnr.wi.gov/org/land/er/sna

Wisconsin State Park System, www.dnr.state.wi.us/org/land/parks

# Directory

## Getting There

### Bus Lines

Greyhound Lines
(800) 231-2222
www.greyhound.com

Jefferson Lines
(800) 767-5333
www.jeffersonlines.com

Indian Trails
(800) 292-3831
www.indiantrails.com

Lamers Bus Lines
(800) 261-6600 or (715) 241-7799
www.golamers.com

### Train

Amtrak
www.amtrak.com

## By the Inland Sea:
## Bayfield Peninsula Area

### Where to Stay

Pinehurst Inn
83645 Highway 13

Bayfield, WI 54814
(715) 779-3676 or (877) 499-7651
www.pinehurstinn.com

Enso Wellness Center and
 Day Spa
83645 Highway 13
Bayfield, WI 54814
(715) 209-5553
www.ensowellnessspa.com

Brittany Cottages at Coole Park
351 Old Fort Road
La Pointe, WI 54850
(715) 747-5023
www.brittanycabins.com

Seagull Bay Motel
325 South Seventh Street
Bayfield, WI 54814
(715) 779-5558
www.seagullbay.com

Island View Inn and Cottages
86720 Island View Lane
Bayfield, WI 54814
(715) 779-5307 or (888) 309-5307
www.islandviewbandb.com

159

*Directory*

Inn on Madeline Island
P.O. Box 93
La Pointe, WI 54850
(800) 822-6315
madisland.com

Bayfield Inn
20 Rittenhouse Avenue
Bayfield, WI 54814
(715) 779-3363 or
   (800) 382-0995
www.bayfieldinn.com

Harbor's Edge Motel
33 North Front Street
Bayfield, WI 54814
(715) 779-3962
www.harborsedgemotel.com

Rittenhouse Inn
301 Rittenhouse Avenue
Bayfield, WI 54814
(715) 779-5111
www.rittenhouseinn.com

Artesian House
84100 Hatchery Road
Bayfield, WI 54814
(715) 779-3338
www.artesianhouse.com

Buffalo Bay Campgrounds and
   Marina
14669 Highway 13
Bayfield, WI 54814
(715) 779-3743
www.ncis.net/bflobay

### Where to Eat

Big Water Cafe and Coffee
   Roasters
117 Rittenhouse Avenue
Bayfield, WI 54814
(715) 779-9619
www.bigwatercoffee.com

Rittenhouse Inn's Landmark Restaurant
301 Rittenhouse Avenue
Bayfield, WI 54814
(715) 779-5111
www.rittenhouseinn.com

Maggie's
257 Manypenny Avenue
Bayfield, WI 54814
(715) 779-5641
www.maggies-bayfield.com

Wild Rice Restaurant
84860 Old San Road
Bayfield, WI 54814
(715) 779-9881
www.wildricerestaurant.com

Ashland Baking Company
212 Chapple Avenue
Ashland, WI 54806
(715) 682-6010
www.ashlandbakingcompany.com

Black Cat Coffeehouse
211 Chapple Avenue
Ashland, WI 54806
(715) 682-3680

Lotta's Lakeside Cafe
1 block from the ferry landing on
   Madeline Island
La Pointe, WI 54850
(715) 747-2033
www.lottascafe.com

### Local Foraging

Bayfield Farmers' Market
Manypenny Avenue and
   Third Street
Bayfield, WI 54814

Washburn Farmers' Market
Bayfield Street
Washburn, WI 54891

Cornucopia Farmers' Market
Town Beach Park, just off Highway 13
Cornucopia, WI 54827

Ashland Area Farmers' Market
200 block of Chapple Avenue
Ashland, WI 54806

Bodin Fisheries
208 Wilson Avenue
Bayfield, WI 54814
(715) 779-3301
www.bodinfisheries.com

Chequamegon Food Co-op
215 Chapple Avenue
Ashland, WI 54806
(715) 682-8251

Apple Hill Orchards
34980 County Road J
Bayfield, WI 54814
(715) 779-5425

Bayfield Apple Company
87540 County Road J
Bayfield, WI 54814
(715) 779-5700
www.bayfieldapple.com

Blue Vista Farm
34045 South County Road J
Bayfield, WI 54814
(715) 779-5400
www.bluevistafarm.com

Erickson Orchard and Country
    Store
86600 Betzold Road
Bayfield, WI 54814
(715) 779-5438
www.ericksonsorchard.com

Good Earth Gardens
87185 County Road J

Bayfield, WI 54814
(715) 779-5564

### What to Do

Apostle Islands National Lakeshore
415 Washington Avenue
Bayfield, WI 54814
(715) 779-3397
www.nps.gov/apis

Living Adventure, Inc.
88260 Highway 13
Bayfield, WI 54814
(715) 779-9503 or (866) 779-9503
livingadventure.com

Inland Sea Kayak Symposium
Lake Superior Water Trail
P.O. Box 145
Washburn, WI 54891
(715) 682-8188
www.inlandsea.org

Dreamcatcher Sailing
100-B Rittenhouse Avenue
Bayfield, WI 54814
(800) 682-1587 or (715) 779-5561
www.dreamcatcher-sailing.com

Bayfield Bike Route
251 Manypenny Avenue
Bayfield, WI 54814
(715) 209-6864 or (715) 779-3132
bayfieldbikeroute.com

Red Cliff Tribal Fish Hatchery
88385 Pike Road Highway 13
Bayfield, WI 54814
(715) 779-3728
redcliff-nsn.gov/divisions/
    Natural Resources/hatchery.htm

Red Cliff Band of Lake Superior
    Chippewa
14669 Highway 13 North

Bayfield, WI 54814
(715) 779-3712
redcliff-nsn.gov

Wolfsong Adventures in Mushing
88265 Happy Hollow Road
Bayfield, WI 54814
(800) 681-9746 or
  (715) 779-5561
www.wolfsongadventures.com

Apostle Islands Sled Dog Race
bayfield.org/festivals_events
  _sled_dog.php

Bayfield Winter Festival
www.bayfieldwinterfestival.com

Bayfield Area Recreation Center
140 South Broad Street
Bayfield, WI 54814
(715) 779-5408
www.bayfieldreccenter.com

Book Across the Bay
P.O. Box 307
Ashland, WI 54806
(715) 682-2500 or
  (800) 284-9484
www.batb.org

Mt. Ashwabay Ski and Recreation
  Area
Ski Hill Road
Bayfield, WI 54814
(715) 779-3227
www.mtashwabay.org

Nourse Sugarbush State Natural Area
dnr.wi.gov/org/land/er/sna/
  index.asp?SNA=534

Madeline Island Ferry Line
(715) 747-2051
www.madferry.com

Big Bay State Park
Madeline Island
(715) 747-6425
www.dnr.state.wi.us/org/land/parks/
  specific/bigbay

Big Bay Sand Spit and Bog State
  Natural Area
dnr.wi.gov/org/land/er/sna/
  index.asp?SNA=156

Northern Great Lakes Visitor
  Center
2 miles west of Ashland at County
  Road G and Highway 2
(715) 685-9983
www.nglvc.org

Red Cliff Pow-wow
redcliff-nsn.gov/Tourism/powwow
  .htm

Bad River Pow-wow
www.glitc.org/web-content/pages/
  pow-wows.html

Native Spirit Gifts and Gallery
37390 Highway 13 North
Bayfield, WI 54814
(715) 779-9550

Woods Hall Craft Shop
Main Street
P.O. Box 196
La Pointe, WI 54850
(715) 747-3943

Madeline Island Historical
  Museum
226 Colonel Woods Avenue
P.O. Box 9
La Pointe, WI 54850
(715) 747-2415
madelineislandmuseum.wisconsin
  history.org

Madeline Island School of the Arts
978 Middle Road
La Pointe, WI 54850
(715) 747-2054
www.madelineartschool.com

Apostle Islands Booksellers
112 Rittenhouse Avenue
Bayfield, WI 54814
(715) 779-0200
www.apostleislandsbooksellers.com

What Goes 'Round
38 South Second Street
Bayfield, WI 54814
(877) 779-5223 or (715) 779-5223

Bayfield Heritage Tours
(715) 779-0299
www.bayfieldheritagetours.com

Lake Superior Big Top Chautauqua
101 West Bayfield Street
Washburn, WI 54891
(715) 373-5552 or (888) 244-8368
www.bigtop.org

Stage North Theater
123 West Omaha Street
Washburn, WI 54891
(715) 373-1194
www.stagenorth.com

Big Water Film Festival
www.bigwaterfilmfestival.org

Sigurd Olson Environmental
    Institute
Northland College
1411 Ellis Avenue
Ashland, WI 54806
(715) 682-1223
www.northland.edu/sigurd-olson-
    environmental-institute-overview-
    .htm

Timeless Timber
2200 East Lake Shore Drive
Ashland, WI 54806
(888) 653-5647
www.timelesstimber.com

## Happy Trails: Cable and Hayward Area

### Where to Stay

Cable Nature Lodge
20100 County Highway M
Cable, WI 54821
(715) 794-2060 or
    (866) 794-2060
www.cablenaturelodge.com

### Where to Eat

The Rookery Pub
20100 County Highway M
Cable, WI 54821
(715) 794-2060 or
    (866) 794-2060

Brick House Cafe
13458 Reynolds Street
Cable, WI 54821
(715) 798-5432
thebrickhousecafe.net

The Original Famous Dave's
9971N Grand Pines Lane
Hayward, WI 54843
(715) 462-3352
www.famousdaveshayward.com

Angry Minnow
10440 Florida Avenue
Hayward, WI 54843
(715) 934-3055
www.angryminnow.com

### Local Foraging

Hayward Mercantile Company
Truly Wisconsin

Truly Delicious Chef Shop
10541 Main Street
Hayward, WI 54843
(715) 634-7179
www.haywardmercantile.com

White Winter Winery
68323 Lea Street
Iron River, WI 54847
(800) 697-2006 or
  (715) 372-5656
www.whitewinter.com

### What to Do

Rock Lake Trail
From Highway 63 in Cable, 7.5 miles
  east on County Road M
www.cambatrails.org/camba-bin/
  show_camba_trails.cgi/?feed
  _trail=Namakagon %20Cluster

Chequamegon-Nicolet National
  Forest
500 Hanson Lake Road
Rhinelander, WI 54501
(715) 362-1300
www.fs.usda.gov; www.stateparks
  .com/chequamegon.html

Porcupine Lake Wilderness Area
Great Divide Ranger District
N22223 Highway 13
Glidden, WI 54527
(715) 264-2511
or
10650 Nyman Avenue
Hayward, WI 54843
(715) 634-4821
www.fs.fed.us/r9/cnnf/rec/wilderness/
  index.html; www.wilderness.net

North Country National Scenic
  Trail
(608) 441-5610
www.nps.gov/noco/index.htm

Rainbow Lake Wilderness Area
Washburn Ranger District
113 Bayfield Street East
Washburn, WI 54891
(715) 373-2667
www.fs.fed.us/r9/cnnf/rec/wilderness/
  index.html; www.wilderness.net

Namekagon River
www.huntfishcampwisconsin.com/
  Namekagon.html

Jack's Canoe and Tube Rental
N7550 Canfield Drive
Trego, WI 54888
(715) 635-3300
www.jackscanoerental.com/index .html

National Park Service Campsites
www.nps.gov/sacn/planyourvisit/
  camping.htm

Down to Earth Tours
46830 Cranberry Lake Road
Gordon, WI 54838
(715) 376-4260
www.downtoearthtours.com

Cable Natural History Museum
13470 County Road M
Cable, WI 54821
(715) 798-3890
www.cablemuseum.org

Wisconsin Canoe Heritage Museum
312 North Front Street
Spooner, WI 54801
(715) 635-5002
www.wisconsincanoeheritage
  museum.com

Chequamegon Area Mountain Bike
  Association (CAMBA)
(715) 798-3599
www.cambatrails.org

Sara Qualey
(715) 798-4842
www.saraqualey.com

Mulberry Street
41410 Highway 63
Cable, WI 54821
(715) 798-4237
www.shopmulberrystreet.com

Chequamegon Fat Tire Festival
P.O. Box 267
Telemark Resort
Cable, WI 54821
(715) 798-3594
www.cheqfattire.com

American Birkebeiner
10527 Main Street
Hayward, WI 54843
(715) 634-5025
www.birkie.com

Telemark Educational Foundation
www.telemarkeducation.com
(877) 798-4718, ext. 547 or
    (715) 798-3999, ext. 547

## Far from the Madding Crowds: Chetek and New Auburn Area

### Where to Stay

Canoe Bay
Chetek, WI 54728
(715) 924-4594, ext. 4 or
    (800) 568-1995, ext. 4
www.canoebay.com

Jacks Lake Bed and Breakfast
30497 138th Street
New Auburn, WI 54757
(715) 967-2593

### Where to Eat

Adventures Restaurant and Pub

2901 College Drive
Rice Lake, WI 54868
(715) 434-4040
www.adventuresrestaurant.com

### Local Foraging

On Twin Lakes Store and Family
    Farm
2522 Twenty-eighth Avenue
Birchwood, WI 54817
(715) 354-3210
www.ontwinlakes.com

Deedon Lake Natural Orchard
552 138th Avenue
Turtle Lake, WI 54889
(715) 986-2757

Viking Brewing Company
Dallas, WI 54733
(715) 837-1824
www.vikingbrewing.com

### What to Do

Mi Zi Zak Kayaks
29588 Highway 40, between
    129th Avenue and 136th Street
New Auburn, WI 54757
(715) 967-2301

Ice Age Interpretive Center
7 miles east of New Auburn and 1.9
    miles east of State Highway 40 on
    County Highway M
dnr.wi.gov/org/land/parks/specific/
    chipmoraine/center.html; www
    .iceagetrail.org

Chippewa Moraine State Recreation
    Area
13394 County Highway M
New Auburn, WI 54757
(715) 967-2800
dnr.wi.gov/org/land/parks/specific/
    chipmoraine

Blue Hills Trail
Bruce, WI 54819
(715) 532-6595
www.bluehillstrail.com

## Spiritual Getaway:
## Clark County Forest Area

### Where to Stay

Christine Center
W8303 Mann Road
Willard, WI 54493
(715) 267-7507
www.christinecenter.org

### Local Foraging

North Hendren Co-op Dairy
W8204 Spencer Road
Willard, WI 54493
(715) 267-6617
www.northhendrenbluecheese.com

Holland's Family Cheese
N13851 Gorman Avenue
Thorp, WI 54771
(715) 669-5230
www.hollandsfamilycheese.com

### What to Do

Mead Lake County Park
W8771 North Lake Road
Willard, WI 54493
(715) 743-5140
http://www.co.clark.wi.us/Clark
    County/Departments/forestryparks/
    ParksCamp/NorthMead.asp

Rock Dam County Park
W10666 Camp Globe Road
Willard, WI 54493
(715) 267-6845
http://www.co.clark.wi.us/Clark
    County/Departments/forestryparks/
    ParksCamp/RockDam.asp

Levis/Trow Mound Recreation
    Area
N1589 Fisher Avenue
Neillsville, WI 54456
www.levismound.com

The Highground
W7031 Ridge Road
Neillsville, WI 54456
(715) 743-4224
www.thehighground.org

## Earth-Friendly Retreat:
## Lake Pepin Area

### Where to Stay

Journey Inn
W3671 200th Avenue
Maiden Rock, WI 54750
(715) 448-2424
www.journeyinn.net

Cottage at Journey Inn
W3675 200th Avenue
Maiden Rock, WI 54750
(715) 448-2424
www.cottageatjourneyinn.net

### Where to Eat

Smiling Pelican Bake Shop
Off Highway 35 in the village
Maiden Rock, WI 54750
(715) 448-3807

Bogus Creek Cafe and Bakery
N2049 Spring Street
Stockholm, WI 54769
(715) 442-5017

Stockholm Pie Company
N2030 Spring Street #1
Stockholm, WI 54769
(715) 442-5505
thestockholmpiecompany.com

A to Z Produce and Bakery
N2956 Anker Lane
Stockholm, WI 54769
www.atozproduceandbakery .com

## Local Foraging

Rush River Produce
W4098 200th Avenue
Maiden Rock, WI 54750
(715) 594-3648
www.rushriverproduce.com

Maiden Rock Orchard
W12266 King Lane
Stockholm, WI 54769
(715) 448-3502
www.maidenrockapples.com

Stockholm General
N2030 #4 Spring Street
Stockholm, WI 54769
(715) 442-9077

Honey Hill Apiary
N469 300th Street
Maiden Rock, WI 54750
(715) 448-2517

Anderson's Farm
N6501 Manore Lane
Arkansaw, WI 54721
(888) 700-FARM [3276]
www.andersonfarm.us

Eau Galle Cheese Factory
N6765 Highway 25
Durand, WI 54736
(715) 283-4276
www.eaugallecheese.com

Blue Gentian Farm
1990 Highway 46
New Richmond, WI 54017
www.bluegentianfarm.com

## What to Do

Lake Pepin Farm and Food Tour
www.lakepepinfarmtour.com;
www.thekitchensage.com

The Palate
W12102 Highway 35
Stockholm, WI 54769
(715) 442-6400
www.thepalate.net

Morgan Coulee Prairie State Natural
Area
dnr.wi.gov/org/land/er/sna/index
.asp?SNA=205

Maiden Rock Bluff State Natural Area
dnr.wi.gov/org/land/er/sna/index
.asp?SNA=410
Rush River Delta State Natural Area
dnr.wi.gov/org/land/er/sna/index
.asp?SNA=202

Abode Gallery
N2030 #3 Spring Street
Stockholm, WI 54769
(715) 442-2266
www.abodegallery.com

Northern Oak Amish Furniture
N2048 Spring Street
Stockholm, WI 54769
(715) 442-6008
northernoakamishfurniture.com

Stockholm Pottery and Mercantile
N2020 Spring Street
Stockholm, WI 54769
(715) 442-9012
www.stockholmpottery.com

A Sense of Place
N2037 Spring Street

Stockholm, WI 54769
(651) 528-9616

Stockholm Art Fair
www.stockholmartfair.org

Fresh Art Fall and Spring Tours
www.freshart.org

## Where Eagles Soar: Upper Mississippi River Area

### Where to Stay

Historic Trempealeau Hotel
11332 Main Street
Trempealeau, WI 54661
(608) 534-6898
www.trempealeauhotel.com

Hawks View Cottages and Lodges
Fountain City, WI 54629
(866) 293-0803 or
    (651) 293-0803
www.hawksview.net

Hotel de Ville
305 North Main Street
Alma, WI 54610
(612) 423-3653
www.hoteldevillealma.com

### Where to Eat

Historic Trempealeau Hotel
11332 Main Street
Trempealeau, WI 54661
(608) 534-6898
www.trempealeauhotel.com

Monarch Tavern
19 North Main Street
Fountain City, WI 54629
(608) 687-4231
monarchtavern.com

Seven Hawks Vineyards
17 North Street
Fountain City, WI 54629
(608) 687-9463 or
    (866) 946-3741
www.sevenhawksvineyards
    .com

Kate and Gracie's
215 North Main Street
Alma, WI 54610
(608) 685-4505
www.kateandgracies.com

The Stone Barn
S685 County Road KK
Nelson, WI 54756
(715) 673-4478
nelsonstonebarn.com

Homemade Cafe
809 Third Street
Pepin, WI 54759
(612) 396-5804
homemadecafe.com

### Local Foraging

Great River Organic Milling
118 South Main Street
Fountain City, WI 54629
(608) 687-9580
www.greatrivermilling.com

Coon Creek Family Farm
Vince and Julie Maro
Mondovi, WI 54755
(715) 834-4547
www.cooncreekfamilyfarm.com

Castle Rock Organic Farms
S13240 Young Road
Osseo, WI 54758
(715) 597-0085
www.castlerockfarms.net

## What to Do

Upper Mississippi River National
  Wildlife and Fish Refuge
51 East Fourth Street
Winona, MN 55987
(507) 452-4232
www.fws.gov/midwest/
  UpperMississippiRiver

Rock in the House
440 Front Street
Fountain City, WI 54629
(608) 687-6106
www.greatriver.com/natural/
  disaster/Rock/rockinhouse.htm

Perrot State Park
W26247 Sullivan Road
Trempealeau, WI 54661
www.dnr.state.wi.us/org/land/
  parks/specific/perrot

Trempealeau National Wildlife Refuge
W28488 Refuge Road
Trempealeau, WI 54661
www.fws.gov/midwest/trempealeau

Buena Vista Park, Overlook and
  Hiking Trails
County Highway E
Alma, WI 54610
(608) 685-3330
www.almawisconsin.com/attractions
  .html

Wings over Alma
118 North Main Street
Alma, WI 54610
(608) 685-3303
www.wingsoveralma.com

Great River Road Bike Trail
(608) 534-6409

www.dnr.state.wi.us/org/land/parks/
  specific/greatriver

Tiffany Wildlife Area
dnr.wi.gov/org/land/wildlife/wildlife
  _areas/tiffany.htm

Tiffany Bottoms State Natural Area
dnr.wi.gov/org/land/er/sna/index
  .asp?SNA=30

Chippewa Valley Motor Car
  Association
www.chippewavalleymotorcar
  association.ellawisc.com

The Prairie Enthusiasts
www.theprairieenthusiasts.com

Great Wisconsin Birding and
  Nature Trail
www.wisconsinbirds.org/trail/
  overview.htm

Audubon Great River Birding Trail
www.greatriverbirding.org/index2
  .php

Prairie Moon Sculpture Garden and
  Museum
S2727 Prairie Moon Road
Cochrane, WI 54622
(608) 687-9874 or
  (608) 687-8252
www.kohlerfoundation.org/rusch.html

The Commercial
305 South Main Street
Alma, WI 54610
(608) 685-4104

BNOX Gold and Iron
404 First Street
Pepin, WI 54759

(715) 442-2201
www.bnoxgold.com

National Eagle Center
50 Pembroke Avenue
Wabasha, MN 55981
(877) 332-4537
www.nationaleaglecenter.org

Fresh Art Fall and Spring Tours
www.freshart.org

## A Trail Runs through It: Upper Saint Croix Valley Area

### Where to Stay

Lake Haven Lodge
2306 243rd Avenue
Cushing, WI 54006
(612) 963-8888
www.lakehavenlodge.com

Wissahickon Farms Country Inn
2263 Maple Drive
Saint Croix Falls, WI 54024
(715) 483-3986
www.wissainn.com

Smoland Prairie Homestead Inn
11658 Highway 70
Grantsburg, WI 54840
(715) 689-2528
www.smolandinn.com

Interstate State Park
Highway 35
P.O. Box 703
Saint Croix Falls, WI 54024
(715) 483-3747
www.dnr.state.wi.us/org/LAND/
   parks/specific/interstate

### Where to Eat

Cafe Wren
2596 Highway 35

Luck, WI 54853
(715) 472-4700
www.cafewren.com

Grecco's on the Saint Croix
115 North Washington
Saint Croix Falls, WI 54024
(715) 483-5003
www.greccos.com

### Local Foraging

Fine Acres Market
102 South Washington
Saint Croix Falls, WI 54024
(715) 483-9918

Natural Alternative Food Co-op
241 Main Street
Luck, WI 54863
(715) 472-8084

Beaver Creek Ranch
12402 Highway 48
Grantsburg, WI 54840
(715) 488-3995

Burnett Dairy Cheese Store
11631 Highway 70
Grantsburg, WI 54840
(715) 689-2748

Chateau Saint Croix Winery and
   Vineyard
1998A Highway 87
Saint Croix Falls, WI 54024
(866) 654-9463
www.chateaustcroix.com

### What to Do

Interstate State Park
Highway 35
Saint Croix Falls, WI 54024
(715) 483-3747
dnr.wi.gov/org/land/parks/specific/
   interstate

Saint Croix National Scenic Riverway
    Visitor Center
401 North Hamilton Street
Saint Croix Falls, WI 54024
(715) 483-2274
www.nps.gov/sacn/index.htm

Wild River Outfitters
15177 Highway 70
Grantsburg, WI 54840
(715) 463-2254
www.wildriverpaddling.com

Gandy Dancer State Trail
www.wnrmag.com/org/land/
    parks/specific/gandydancer

Straight Lake State Park
(715) 483-3747
dnr.wi.gov/org/land/parks/specific/
    straightlake

Crex Meadows Wildlife Area
102 East Crex Avenue
Grantsburg, WI 54850
(715) 463-2739
www.crexmeadows.org

Brandt Pines Ski Trail
dnr.wi.gov/forestry/stateforests/
    SF-Knowles/brandt_pines.htm

Natural Resources Foundation
    of Wisconsin
www.wisconservation.org

Saint Croix Festival Theatre
210 North Washington Street
Saint Croix Falls, WI 54024
(715) 483-3387 or (888) 887-6002
www.festivaltheatre.org

Saint Croix Falls Public Library
230 South Washington Street
Saint Croix Falls, WI 54024

(715) 483-1777
www.stcroixfallslibrary.org

Saint Croix Scenic Coalition
www.stcroixsceniccoalition.org

Saint Croix Scenic Byway
www.stcroixscenicbyway.org

Earth Arts of the Upper Saint Croix
    Valley
Spring Art Tour and Fall Art Salon
www.earthartswi.org

West Denmark Lutheran Church
2478 170th Street
Luck, WI 54853
(715) 472-2383

Luhr/Björnson Artworks
241 North Washington Street
Saint Croix Falls, WI 54024
(715) 483-9612

Blackberry Hills
2150 220th Street
Saint Croix Falls, WI 54024
(715) 483-9434
www.blackberryhills.com

Mrs. I's Yarn Parlor
201 Third Street
Osceola, WI 54020
(715) 294-4775
www.yarnparlor.com

Saint Croix Wild Rice Pow-wow
www.stcciw.com; danbury.stcroix
    casino.com

Community Homestead
501 280th Street
Osceola, WI 54020
(715) 294-3038
www.communityhomestead.org

## Renewable Energy Pioneers: Amherst Area

### Where to Stay

Artha Sustainable Living Center
9784 County Road K
Amherst, WI 54406
(715) 824-3463
www.arthaonline.com

Amherst Riverdance
5051 Keener Road
Amherst, WI 54406
(715) 824-7151
www.amherstriverdance.com/
    cabin.html

### Where to Eat

Morning Star Coffee and Bistro
102 South Main Street
Amherst, WI 54406
(715) 824-2200
www.morningstarcoffeeandbistro.com

New Village Bakery
127 North Main Street
Amherst, WI 54406
(715) 824-7654

Central Waters Brewing Company
351 Allen Street
Amherst, WI 54406
(715) 824-2739
centralwaters.com

### What to Do

Midwest Renewable Energy Fair
Midwest Renewable Energy Association
7558 Deer Road
Custer, WI 54423
(715) 592-6595
www.the-mrea.org

Festival of Chocolate
www.festivalofchocolate.org

Pickerel Lake State Natural Area
dnr.wi.gov/org/land/er/sna/index
    .asp?SNA=227

Richard A. Hemp State Fishery Area
dnr.wi.gov/org/land/wildlife/wildlife
    _areas/temp/rjhemp.htm

Heartland Bike and Nordic Ski Club
www.heartlandclub.org

Iola Scandinavia Fitness and Aquatic
    Center
445 South Jackson Street
Iola, WI 54945
(715) 445-2411, ext. 317

Tomorrow River State Trail
dnr.wi.gov/org/land/parks/specific/
    tomorrowriv/index.html

Lettie's River Run
lettiesriverrun.org

Standing Rocks Park
www.co.portage.wi.us/parks/standing
    RocksPark.shtm

Tomorrow River Gallery
182 South Main Street
Amherst, WI 54406
(715) 321-2142
www.tomorrowrivergallery.com

Hidden Studios Art Tour
www.hiddenstudiosarttour.com

Wisconsin Wool Exchange
123 Main Street
Amherst, WI 54406
(715) 824-3358
www.wisconsinwoolexchange.com

Rising Star Mill
3190 County Highway Q

Nelsonville, WI 54458
(715) 445-2954
www.pchswi.org/events/mill
 _events.htm

## Arts and Orchards of the Door Peninsula: Door County

### *Where to Stay*

Lodgings at Pioneer Lane
9998 Pioneer Lane
Ephraim, WI 54211
(800) 588-3565 or
 (920) 854-7656
www.lodgingsatpioneerlane.com

Whitefish Bay Farm
3831 Clark Lake Road (County
 Road WD)
Sturgeon Bay, WI 54235
(920) 743-1560
whitefishbayfarm.com

### *Where to Eat*

The Cookery
4135 Highway 42/Main Street
Fish Creek, WI 54212
(920) 868-3634
www.cookeryfishcreek.com

Mr. Helsinki
4164 Main Street
Fish Creek, WI 54212
(920) 868-9898
www.mrhelsinki.com

Waterfront
10961 North Highway 42
Sister Bay, WI 54234
(920) 854-5491
www.jjswaterfront.com

### *Local Foraging*

Greens N Grains
7821 Highway 42

Egg Harbor, WI 54209
(920) 868-9999
www.greens-n-grains.com

Harbor Ridge Winery
4690 Rainbow Ridge Court
Egg Harbor, WI 54209
(920) 868-4321
www.harborridgewinery.com

EcoDoor
9331 Spring Road, Unit B17
Fish Creek, WI 54212
(920) 868-5400
www.ecodoorliving.com

Seaquist Orchards
Highway 42 between Ellison Bay and
 Sister Bay
(920) 854-4199 or (800) 732-8850
www.seaquistorchards.com/
 contact.php

### *What to Do*

Concerts in the Park
Harbor View Park
Egg Harbor, WI 54209
eggharbordoorcounty.org

Peg Egan Performing Arts Center
Egg Harbor Eames Cherry View Park
7840 Church Street
Egg Harbor, WI 54209
(920) 493-5979
www.theartofmusiclive.com/
 pegegan.html

Door County Trolley Wine Tour
(920) 868-1100
doorcountytrolley.com

Orchard Country Winery and
 Market
9197 Highway 42
Fish Creek, WI 54212

(920) 868-3479
www.orchardcountry.com

Door County Lighthouses
4639 Orchard Road
Egg Harbor, WI 54209
www.dclighthouseinn.com

Ephraim Wetlands Preserve
rustic entrance at 9820 Water Street
    (Highway 42)
www.ephraim-doorcounty.com/
    parks/wetlands.htm

Ridges Sanctuary
P.O. Box 152
Baileys Harbor, WI 54202
(920) 839-2802 or (920) 839-1101
www.ridgesanctuary.org

Edge of Park
Park Entrance Road
Fish Creek, WI 54212
(920) 868-3344
www.edgeofpark.com

Peninsula State Park
9462 Shore Road
Fish Creek, WI 54212
(920) 868-3258
dnr.wi.gov/org/land/parks/specific/
    peninsula/

Newport State Park
475 County Highway NP
Ellison Bay WI 54210
(920) 854-2500
dnr.wi.gov/org/land/parks/specific/
    newport

Nor Door Sport and Cycle
4007 Highway 42
Fish Creek, WI 54212
(920) 868-2275
Nordoorsports.com

Potawatomi State Park
3740 County Road PD
Sturgeon Bay, WI 54235
(920) 746-2890
dnr.wi.gov/org/land/parks/specific/
    Potawatomi

Friends of Potawatomi State Park
www.runwild.org/friends.htm

Whitefish Dunes State Park
275 Clark Lake Road
Sturgeon Bay, WI 54235
(920) 823-2400
dnr.wi.gov/org/land/parks/specific/
    whitefish/

Rock Island State Park
1924 Indian Point Road
Washington Island, WI 54246
dnr.wi.gov/org/land/parks/specific/
    rockisland

Friends of Rock Island State Park
www.uniontel.net/~cmarlspc/

Door County Kayak Tours
8442 State Highway 42
Fish Creek, WI 54212
(920) 868-1400 or (920) 344-6641
www.doorcountykayaktours.com

Kayaking Adventures Shop
4690 Rainbow Ridge Court
Egg Harbor, WI 54209
(920) 868-4321
www.kayakingadventuresdoor
    county.com

Bay Shore Outdoor Store
2457 South Bay Shore Drive
State Highway 42
Sister Bay, WI 54234
(920) 854-7598
www.kayakdoorcounty.com

Ephraim Kayak Center
South Shore Pier
Ephraim, WI 54211
(920) 854-4336
www.kayakdoorcounty.com/sailing
.htm

Door County Festival of Nature
The Sanctuary, Inc.
P.O. Box 152
Baileys Harbor, WI 54202
(920) 839-2802
www.ridgessanctuary.org/festivalof
nature.aspx

Peninsula School of Art
3900 County Road F
Fish Creek, WI 54212
(920) 868-3455
www.peninsulaartschool.com

Door County Plein Air Festival
www.doorcountypleinair.com

Door County Half Marathon
Niclolet Bay 5K
www.doorcountyhalfmarathon
.com

Ecology Sports
10904 Highway 42
Sister Bay, WI 54234
(800) 274-6731

TR Pottery
4133 Main Street
Fish Creek, WI 54212
(920) 868-1024
www.Trpottery.com

Edgewood Orchard Galleries
4140 Peninsula Players Road
Fish Creek, WI 54212
(920) 868-3579
www.edgewoodorchard.com

Gloria Hardiman
9098 County Road F
Fish Creek, WI 54212
(920) 839-2693
www.gloriahardiman.com

Clay Bay Pottery
11650 Highway 42
Ellison Bay, WI 54210
(920) 854-5027
www.claybaypottery.net

American Folklore Theatre
P.O. Box 273
Fish Creek, WI 54212
(920) 854-6117
www.folkloretheatre.com

Birch Creek Music Performance
Center
3821 County Road E
Egg Harbor, WI 54209
(920) 868-3763
www.birchcreek.org

Door Community Auditorium
3926 Highway 42
Fish Creek, WI 54212
(920) 868-2728
www.dcauditorium.org

Door Shakespeare
P.O. Box 351
Baileys Harbor, WI 54202
(920) 839-1500
www.doorshakespeare.com

Isadoora Theatre Company
P.O. Box 734
Fish Creek, WI 54212
(920) 493-3667
www.isadoora.com

Midsummer's Music
P.O. Box 1004

Sister Bay, WI 54234
(920) 854-7088
www.midsummermusic.com

Peninsula Music Festival
3045 Cedar Street
Ephraim, WI 54211
(920) 854-4060
www.musicfestival.com

Peninsula Players
4351 Peninsula Players Road
Fish Creek, WI 54212
(920) 868-3287
www.peninsulaplayers.com

Third Avenue Playhouse
239 North Third Avenue
Sturgeon Bay, WI 54235
(920) 743-1760
www.thirdavenueplayhouse.com

The Clearing
12171 Garrett Bay Road
Ellison Bay, WI 54210
(920) 854-4088 or
   (877) 854-3225
www.theclearing.org

## Chequamegon-Nicolet Forest, Wisconsin's National Treasure: Eagle River and Presque Isle Area

### Where to Stay

Lake Forest Resort and Club
1531 Golf View Road
Eagle River, WI 54521
(715) 479-2455
www.lakeforestresort.com

Alpine Resort
7151 Crab Lake Road
Presque Isle, WI 54557
(715) 686-2800 or (877) 888-6805
www.Alpine-Resort.com

Trees for Tomorrow
519 Sheridan Street East
Eagle River, WI 54521
(715) 479-6456
www.treesfortomorrow.com

### Where to Eat

Riverstone Restaurant and Tavern
219 North Railroad Street
Eagle River, WI 54521
(715) 479-8462
www.riverstonerestaurant.com

### Local Foraging

Grass Roots Health Foods
3440 Highway 70 East
Eagle River, WI 54521
(715) 479 6299
www.grassrootsonline.com

### What to Do

Anvil National Recreation Trail
www.fs.fed.us/r9/cnnf/rec/wilderness/
   index.html

Three Eagle Trail
P.O. Box 297
Three Lakes, WI 54562
www.3eagletrail.com

Nicolet Wheel-A-Way
Three Lakes, WI 54562
(715) 546-3344 or
   (800) 972-6103
www.threelakes.com

Turtle-Flambeau Flowage
www.turtleflambeauflowage
   wisconsin.info

Manitowish River Trail
www.mercercc.com/recreation/canoe-
   kayaking.html

Catherine Wolter Wilderness Area
East Bay Road

Presque Isle, WI 54557
(715) 682-5789
www.nature.org/ourinitiatives/
regions/northamerica/united
states/wisconsin/index.htm

Three Lakes Do It Best Hardware
1812 Superior Street
Three Lakes, WI 54562
(715) 546-3680
www.threelakeshardware.com

Hawk's Nest Canoe Outfitters
1761 County Road C
Saint Germain, WI 54558
(800) 688-7471 or (715) 542-2300
hawksnestcanoe.com

Rugger's Landing
5643N Highway 51
Mercer, WI 54547
(715) 476-2530
www.mercerwi.com/ruggerland

Guido Rahr Sr. Tenderfoot Forest
Reserve
www.nature.org/ourinitiatives/
regions/northamerica/united
states/wisconsin/index.htm

Circle of Life Studio and Gallery
3720 Gaffney Drive
Eagle River, WI 54521
(715) 479-9737
Circleoflifestudio.com

Northwoods Art Tour
P.O. Box 95
McNaughton, WI 54543
(715) 277-4224
www.northwoodsarttour.com.

Vilas County Historical Museum
217 Main Street
Sayner, WI 54560
(715) 542-3388

George W. Brown Jr. Ojibwe Museum
and Cultural Center
603 Peace Pipe Road
Lac du Flambeau, WI 54538
(715) 588-3333
www.lacduflambeauchamber.com/
attractions.htm

Waswagoning
2750 County Road H
Lac du Flambeau, WI 54538
(715) 588-3560
www.waswagoning.us

Golden Eagle Farms
Highway 70 West
Lac du Flambeau, WI 54538
www.lacduflambeauchamber.com/
attractions.htm

## Wisconsin's Waterfall Capital: Marinette and Langlade Counties

### Where to Stay

Bear Paw Outdoor Adventure Resort
N3494 Highway 55
White Lake, WI 54491
(715) 882-3502

Kosir's Rapid Rafts
W14073 County Road C
Silver Cliff, WI 54104
(715) 757-3431
www.kosirs.com

Rapids Resort
W14091 County Road C
Silver Cliff, WI 54104
(715) 757-3358
ironsnowshoe.com/rapidsresort/
activities.html

Twelve Foot Falls Park
West of Highway 141, off of Highway 8
therealnorth.com; www.marinette
county.com

## Where to Eat

Amy's at Woodhaven
16330 Thelen Road
Mountain, WI 54149
(715) 276-COOK [2665]
www.amysatwoodhaven.com

Bear Paw Pub
N3494 Highway 55
White Lake, WI 54491
(715) 882-3502

Pines Supper Club
15375 County Road W
Crivitz, WI 54114
(715) 276-6226

Mickey-Lu Bar-B-Q
1710 Marinette Avenue
Marinette, WI 54143
(715) 735-7721

Schussler's Supper Club
W3529 County Road B
Peshtigo, WI 54157
(715) 582-3956

## Local Foraging

Oneida Museum
W892 County Road EE
De Pere, WI 54115
(920) 869-2768
www.oneidanation.org/museum

Tsyunhehkwa
139 Riverdale Drive
Oneida WI 54155
(920) 869-2718
www.oneidanation.org/tsyunhehkwa/
   page.aspx?id=3896

Oneida Apple Orchard
3976 West Mason Street
Oneida, WI 54155

(920) 869-2468
www.oneidanation.org/orchard/
   page.aspx?id=548

Tsyunhehkwa Natural Retail Store
Ridgeview Plaza, Suite 8
3759 West Mason Street
Oneida, WI 54155
(920) 497-5821
www.oneidanation.org/tsyunhehkwa/
   page.aspx?id=3900

Oneida Farmers' Market
Oneida One-Stop
W180 Highway 54
Oneida, WI 54155
(920) 869-6294
www.oneidanation.org/ocifs/
   page.aspx?id=532

Oneida Nation Farms
N6010 County Road C
Seymour, WI 54165
www.oneidanation.org/farm

Pleasant View Orchard
W6050 Chapman Road
Niagara, WI 54141
(715) 927-2050
www.pleasantvieworchard.com

Kellner Back Acre Garden
5561 Cooperstown Road
Denmark, WI 54208
(920) 265-5361
www.kellnerbackacregarden .com

Crivitz Farmers' Market
913 Mira Avenue
Crivitz, WI 54114
(715) 927-2330

Green Bay Farmers' Market
North Monroe Avenue between
   Cherry and Pine Streets

Green Bay, WI 54301
(920) 448-3030

Green Bay West Festival Foods
   Farmer Market
2250 West Mason Street
Green Bay, WI 54303
(920) 434-0730

Green Bay East Side Festival Foods
   Farmer Market
3534 Steffens Court
Green Bay, WI 54311
(920) 434-0730

Marinette Farmers Market
Merchant Park
Main and Wells Streets
Marinette, WI 54143
(715) 732-5139

### What to Do

Menominee Indian Cultural
   Museum
W2908 Tribal Office Loop Road
P.O. Box 910
Keshena, WI 54135
(715) 799-5258
www.menominee-nsn.gov

Shotgun Eddy
N2765 Highway 55
White Lake, WI 54491
(715) 882-4461
www.shotguneddy.com

Marinette County Parks
1926 Hall Avenue
Marinette, WI 54143
(715) 732-7533
www.marinettecounty.com/parks/

Peshtigo River State Forest
N10008 Paust Lane
Crivitz, WI 54114

(715) 757-3965
dnr.wi.gov/forestry/stateforests/
   SF-Peshtigo

Thunder Mountain County Park
(715) 732-7530
therealnorth.com; www.marinette
   county.com

## Enter, Northwoods: Rhinelander Area

### Where to Stay

Holiday Acres
4060 South Shore Drive
Rhinelander, WI 54501
holidayacres.com

### Where to Eat

Golden Harvest
627 Coon Street
Rhinelander, WI 54501
(715) 369-5266

Country Seed
210 East Anderson Street
Rhinelander, WI 54501
(715) 362-7333
www.countryseednaturalfoods.com

Joe's Pasty Shop
123 Randall Avenue
Rhinelander, WI 54501
(715) 369-1224
www.ilovepasties.com

### Local Foraging

Hodag Farmers' Market
Pioneer Park
Rhinelander, WI 54501
(715) 282-5656

### What to Do

Riverrun Center for the Arts
McNaughton, WI 54543

(715) 277-4224
www.riverrunarts.com

Nicolet Area Technical College
5364 College Drive
Rhinelander, WI 54501
(715) 365-4410 or (800) 544-3039
www.nicoletcollege.edu

Sokaogon Chippewa Community
Mole Lake
Crandon, WI 54520
(715) 478-3830
www.sokaogonchippewa.com

Bearskin-Hiawatha State Trail
dnr.wi.gov/org/land/parks/specific/
    bearskin; www.northwoods
    biking.com/vilasmaps/lac
    flambeau.htm

## Quiet Waters: Waupaca Area

### Where to Stay

Crystal River Inn Bed and Breakfast
E1369 Rural Road
Waupaca, WI 54981
(715) 258-5333 or (800) 236-5789
www.crystalriver-inn.com

Hartman Creek State Park
N2480 Hartman Creek Road
Waupaca, WI 54981
(715) 258-2372
www.dnr.state.wi.us/org/LAND/
    parks/specific/hartman

### Where to Eat

Freckled Frogg
N2729 County Road QQ
Waupaca, WI 54981
(715) 258-7363

Chez Marché Cafe
108 South Main Street

Waupaca, WI 54981
(715) 281-7431

### Local Foraging

The Bookcellar
110 South Main Street
Waupaca, WI 54981
(715) 258-2555

Waupaca Book Festival
www.waupacalibrary.org/book
    festival/2010

Waupaca Farm Market
Public Square on East Fulton Street
Waupaca, WI 54981
www.waupacafarmmarket.org

Waupaca Strawberry Fest
www.waupacaareachamber.com/
    sbf.html

King Berry Farm
E2076 King Road
Waupaca, WI 54981
(715) 258-6055
www.kingberryfarm.com

### What to Do

Ice Age Trail
www.iceagetrail.org

Emmons Creek Barrens State
    Natural Area
dnr.wi.gov/org/land/er/sna/index
    .asp?SNA=365

Weller Store
E1382 Main Street
Village of Rural
Waupaca, WI 54981
(715) 256-9668
www.wellerstore.com

Old Red Mill
N2190 County Road K

Waupaca, WI 54981
(715) 258-7385

Myklebust Lake State Natural Area
dnr.wi.gov/org/land/er/sna/index
.asp?SNA=179

Arts on the Square
www.waupacaarts.org

Hidden Studios Art Tour
www.hiddenstudiosarttour.com

# Where the Wisconsin River and Farmers Won't Be Ignored: Wausau and Stevens Point Area

### Where to Stay

Stewart Inn
521 Grant Street
Wausau, WI 54403
(715) 849-5858 or
 (715) 571-1646
www.stewartinn.com

A Victorian Swan on Water
1716 Water Street
Stevens Point, WI 54481
(800) 454-9886 or
 (715) 345-0595
www.victorianswan.com

### Where to Eat

Downtown Grocery
607 Third Street
Wausau, WI 54403
(715) 848-9800
www.downtowngrocery.com

Back When Cafe
606 North Third Street
Wausau, WI 54403
(715) 848-5668
www.backwhencafe.com/
 information.html

@1800
Sentry Insurance Headquarters
1800 Northpoint Drive
Stevens Point, WI 54481
(715) 346-1800

Emy J's
1009 First Street
Stevens Point, WI 54481
(715) 345-0471

Adventure 212
Bistro 212
3217 John Joanis Drive
Stevens Point, WI 54482
(715) 343-0212
www.adventure212.com/index.php

CPS Cafe
College of Professional Studies Building
1901 Fourth Avenue
Stevens Point, WI 54481
(715) 346-2830
www.uwsp.edu/hphd/sites/Cafe/
 cpsCafe.shtm

### Local Foraging

Moonshadow Farm
(715) 675-6588
www.downtowngrocery.com/farm.php

Stevens Point Area Co-op
Earthcrust Bakery
633 Second Street
Stevens Point, WI 54481
(715) 341-1555 or (715) 341-4155
spacoop.com

Mullins Cheese
598 Seagull Drive
Mosinee, WI 54455
(715) 693-3205
www.mullinscheese.net

Wisconsin Dairy State Cheese Company
6860 Highway 34

Rudolph, WI 54475
(715) 435-3144

Gifts from the Good Earth
  Farm
10431 Mayflower Road
Milladore, WI 54454
(715) 652-3520
www.goodearthfarms.com

Stoney Acres Farms
7002 Rangeline Road
Athens, WI 54411
www.stoneyacresfarm.net

Maplewood Garden
680 Highway 49
Elderon, WI 54427
(715) 454-6609

Central Rivers Farmshed
www.farmshed.org

**What to Do**

Whitewater Park
200 River Drive
Wausau, WI 54403

Rib Mountain State Park
4200 Park Road
Wausau, WI 54401
(715) 842-2522
www.dnr.state.wi.us/org/land/
  parks/specific/ribmt

Granite Peak Ski Hill
3605 North Mountain Road
Wausau, WI 54402
(715) 845-2846
www.skigranitepeak.com

Mountain Bay Bike Trail
www.trailsfromrails.com/mountain
  _bay_trail.htm

Nine Mile Forest
8704 Red Bud Road
Wausau, WI 54401
(715) 261-1550
www.co.marathon.wi.us/infosubcon
  .asp?dep=25&sid=7

Wausau Wheelers
www.wausauwheelers.org

Green Circle Trail
greencircletrail.org

George W. Mead Wildlife Area
S2148 County Road S
Milladore, WI 54454
(715) 457-6771
www.meadwildlife.org

Ruesch Century Farm
1031 Weeping Willow Drive
Wisconsin Rapids, WI 54494
(715) 424-4468
www.organic-cranberries.com

Performing Arts Foundation Artsblock
401 North Fourth Street
Wausau, WI 54403
(715) 842-0988
www.grandtheater.org

Leigh Yawkey Woodson Art Museum
700 North Twelfth Street
Wausau, WI 54403
(715) 845-7010
www.lywam.org/information

# Index

*Numbers in italics refer to photos. All locations are in Wisconsin unless otherwise noted.*